The Relational Database Advisor
Elements of PC Database Design

The Relational Database Advisor
Elements of PC Database Design

Kimberly Maughan Saunders

Windcrest®/McGraw-Hill

To my husband and family:
without your support, this endeavor would have been
more of the agony and less of the ecstasy (really, it's coming).

FIRST EDITION
FIRST PRINTING

© 1992 by **Windcrest Books**, an imprint of TAB Books.
TAB Books is a division of McGraw-Hill, Inc.
The name "Windcrest" is a registered trademark of TAB Books.

Library of Congress Cataloging-in-Publication Data

Saunders, Kimberly Maughan.
    The relational database advisor : elements of PC database design /
  by Kimberly Maughan Saunders.
        p. cm.
    Includes index.
    ISBN 0-8306-2500-3 :
    1. Data base design. I. Title.
  QA76.9.D26S28   1991   91-21821
  005.75'—dc20   CIP

TAB Books offers software for sale. For information and a catalog, please contact
TAB Software Department, Blue Ridge Summit, PA 17294-0850.

Acquisitions Editor: Ron Powers
Book Editor: Steven L. Burwen
Managing Editor: Sandra L. Johnson
Production: Katherine G. Brown
Series Design: Jaclyn J. Boone
Cover: Sandra Blair Design and Brent Blair Photography, Harrisburg, PA   WT1

Contents

PART 2. DESIGNING A NORMAL DATABASE

Acknowledgments

I would like to express my thanks to Genie Logan for being my reality check, to Martin Rudy for his ongoing support of my professional growth, to Karen Maughan for keeping telephone in hand, and most especially to Paul Maughan for his picky, confrontational, and absolutely wonderful help from beginning to end (oh, and thanks for being a great father, too).

Introduction

The challenge is to use the database in front of you to figure out the answer to your current problem. You might need to decide to hire new staff. You might need to evaluate the growth your business has undergone in the past year in order to project next year's growth. You might need to give your accountant a payroll summary to ensure that your quarterly tax payments are accurate. Perhaps you need to track sales, to manage your contacts with your clients more efficiently, to make your patients' records more accessible, or to plan your schedule more than a day in advance.

What you really need is a way to compile, analyze, and present the information you use in a way that makes the solution to your problem apparent. You need more than a simple database—you need help in making a decision.

If your business is very small, the information you use might be limited in scope. You might only have a single employee, two sales per week, or ten patients total. The help you need might be as close as a $4.99 calculator. You can rack up the numbers, jot down the results, pull out last year's single-page history, and be done with it. Your decision might be obvious even without performing a single calculation. After all, the human mind has powerful analytical abilities. It can assess intuitively the value of great amounts of information.

In today's business world, the likelihood that a single mind could keep track of all the pertinent information is slim. Even if all the details come easily to mind, are the implications of those details as clear? Can you turn your information into *information of value*, without help? Information of value is information that makes a decision simple.

Another fact to consider is that decision-making is time-sensitive. Speed is crucial. Customers rely on an immediate response: will you extend me credit so I can buy this from you? When can I make my next appointment to see you? Where do I put my money when the term of this

CD expires? If you don't provide answers quickly, your customer might go elsewhere. Even if you can do the analysis in your mind or with a calculator, can you do it fast enough?

The computer age

You've been surrounded by computers for years. Still, the vision of your computer as a decision-making tool is vague, and understandably so. No computer vendor is likely to provide you with the details on how you can make your computer do what you need it to do. There are so many elements that make up a computer that the vendors have almost unlimited finger-pointing ability: you aren't getting what you want because of the hardware, the software, the operating system, the application, the hard disk, a memory problem, corrupted files, etc.

True, all of these elements must work together in order to solve your problem: to deliver information of value. However, what is missing from the list is you and the knowledge that you must possess in order to tell the computer to do what you need. You must direct a computer just as you must punch the right keys on a calculator in order to arrive at the correct answer. Instructing a calculator can be simple; instructing a computer rarely is.

The problem is that a computer does not speak the same language that you do. Making the leap from your own thought processes to the manipulation of computer-based information is no easy task. There is a process involved, a certain skill and art to making the translation from what you do to what a computer does.

You and the computer might work with the same information: names and addresses, customers and invoices, patients and records. However, where you have the ability to analyze and understand information from many sources presented in a variety of ways, the computer is limited to storing and manipulating the facts with a predefined method. You can understand information presented in a book, through a videotape, over the telephone, on a napkin, in a conversation. The computer can deal only with information within the confines of very specific rules.

Laying the ground rules

Computer software is intended to help translate your information into and back from the data that the computer actually stores and manipulates. As with any communication between two different languages, the translation must work two ways. Your information first requires translation into computer data (sometimes called *input*). Then the computer's data must be translated in order for you to understand it (sometimes called *output*—see Fig. I-1). Different kinds of software help in the input, storage, manipulation, and output of different kinds of information. The information can range from the relatively simple to the very complex, and thus so can the software.

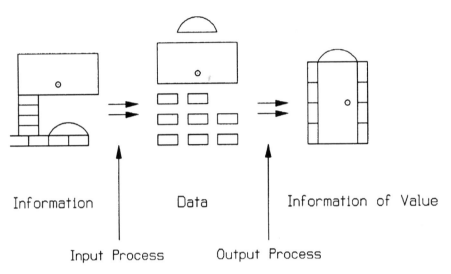

Information   Data   Information of Value

Input Process   Output Process

I-1   The goal of a database.

Word-processing software helps translate a written document into a computer-based information. A typed letter and a simple word-processed document are fairly similar. You usually can begin to use a word processor without a lot of fuss; a few basic PC skills such as knowing how to save and to print allow you to be productive immediately. In this case, the translation from what you do to what the computer does is not a big leap.

More complex information requires more complex software. If instead of keeping track of documents, you must keep track of numbers, your word processor will be inadequate, because no word processor is designed to do that kind of job. You might have settled on a spreadsheet as the appropriate software for your needs. Spreadsheet software allows you to translate more complex information, such as that contained in a chart, into facts that the computer can store and manipulate. The translation required by a spreadsheet is more complicated than that of a word processor. In this instance, the information being translated goes beyond simple words into facts that are related to a structure (the cells in a spreadsheet).

Database software is intended to translate even more complex real-world information into computer-based data. The simplest database software is much like spreadsheet software, but the more sophisticated relational database software also can translate relationships between the different information into computer-based facts. A relational database can help you keep track of a variety of customer information, not only their names and addresses. This data could include which products that customer buys; the age and sex of a patient, and also the details of each and every contact that patient has had with you; the books in your library, who checks out the books, and who checked out which book when.

A database software's ability to translate this more complex kind of information into computer-based data is what makes it powerful, but database software power depends totally on your ability to wield it. Even the easiest-to-use database software expects you to understand how to organize your information before you start. The organization you create before you even turn on the computer, before you input any of your information, will make or break the software's ability to do what it was designed to do. If you expect database software to help you make decisions, you must first understand how to direct it to do so. This book was created to help you understand how to do exactly that.

Directing database software to aid in decision-making begins with the design of the database that the software will act upon. That design process has long been obscured by database software vendors. In their claims of being easy-to-use, the vendors have ignored the very real assumptions that database software, and relational database software in particular, are based upon. The vendors have ignored the need for the users of their products to understand just how data structures are modelled, and thus effectively have excluded the nonprogrammer from ever getting full use from any database software product.

Creating a database design

Database design is a process that should result in a blueprint for building a database. A blueprint for a house specifies such information as the overall dimensions of the house, the sizes of the rooms, the positions of doorways and windows, and the intended use for each room. The blueprint includes essentially all the specifics that will allow a builder to go to work. A database design should achieve the same level of detail. Without specifics, the database "builder" will be unable either to conceive the overall picture or to understand how each part will relate to any other part. The result could well be chaos.

Remember, your goal is to use the computer to help you make decisions. So the first step in defining a database is to outline the overall dimensions of your application. An *application* includes not only the database design but also the directions for how you intend to apply—to use—the database. This can be as simple as a description of the input and output you need for your database system.

Part 1, "Preparing to design a database" (chapters 1 through 3), is intended to give you an overview of the database design process. Chapter 1 addresses in detail the concept of an application and its various elements. Chapter 2 focuses on the steps of the database design process and reviews the basic terminology used by database products, identifying key concepts that will help ensure your success in developing your own design. Chapter 3 provides a series of snapshots of the process, essentially a quick walk-through of a real database design from beginning to end.

Part 2, "Designing a normal database" (chapters 4 through 7), addresses the issues involved in designing a database to take full advantage of the power of relational theory (through normalization—the process of making your database conform to the theory). Chapters 4, 5, and 6 step through the process of table development. Specifically, chapter 4 looks at big-picture considerations, while chapters 5 and 6 analyze the specifics of designing a field and modelling the relationships between tables. Chapter 7 briefly reviews the importance of data integrity and addresses the issue of how to ensure that the data stored in your tables is accurate and the relationships between the tables are valid.

Part 3, "Optimizing a database design" (chapters 8 through 10), addresses the issues involved in fine-tuning a database design. Chapter 8 is an overview of the issues specifically involved in realizing a design. (A *realized design* is one that acknowledges and incorporates the database environment into the database design.) Environmental factors addressed include an assessment of your hardware and network configurations. Chapter 8 also gives you an opportunity to evaluate the "relationality" of your database software, i.e., how well it measures up against the relational model. Finally, chapter 8 touches on some of the issues involved in using a database design actually to produce output.

Chapter 9 addresses the overall concept of performance. How is the speed of a database measured? When is the speed with which a database works an issue? Under what circumstances should you modify a design to take speed into consideration? What can you do to a database design in order to maximize speed?

Finally, chapter 10 addresses the issue of costs. What are the expenses that you reasonably can expect to be associated with the development of a database? Where are the hidden costs, and how can they be avoided? The cost of a database, and specifically of the design process, is evaluated both from a time and dollars-spent standpoint.

Case studies and conventions

Four case studies will be developed as you move through this book. Each addresses a different type of database requirement. Case study 1 reflects the need of a sole proprietor to keep track of time-and-billing matters; case study 2 addresses the requirement of a purchasing group within a large corporation to deal with purchase-order management; case study 3 takes a look at the need of a small zoo to track animals for breeding purposes; and case study 4 deals with a simple list intended to keep track of an individual's depreciable assets.

The intent of the case studies is to help you find your niche—which case study deals with a problem most like the one you're interested in—and focus on it. You'll find the examples most helpful if you identify the case study that fits your needs and follow it through from beginning to end. An issue highlighted especially well by one of the case studies normally is addressed in the body of the text as well, so don't be concerned that you'll miss something important if you don't keep track of them all. A complete database design for each case study can be found in the appendix.

Key concepts and important terms used throughout the book are highlighted with a special *key* icon. The first time the concept or term is defined, the definition is highlighted in the text.

oops!   Mistakes that are made within each case study are marked clearly and identified with a separate mistake icon and a description of the mistake that was made. Each case study is identified with an icon, so that you can quickly refer to the choice of greatest interest to you.

Case study 1: RTS

Type of business: financial planning sole proprietorship.

Employees: 1 full-time, 1 part-time.

Statement of purpose. This financial planner has a need to keep track of what he does and when. He needs to manage his spent time from a historical perspective for billing purposes, and he also needs a way to help him schedule his future time commitments. In addition, he needs to keep better tabs on his client contacts, including who he has talked to, when the contact took place, what recommendations he made, and what follow-up was required.

Case study 2: EB

Type of business: purchasing group within a large retail corporation.
Employees: 11 full-time (within the group).
Statement of purpose. The purchasing group of a nationwide retail sales company needs to manage the process of buying non-merchandise supplies for their stores and corporate entities. The group processes requests for supplies that are submitted by various users, which then forward these requests to a vendor or to a corporate warehouse location as indicated.

 Case study 3: MH

Type of business: small zoo
Employees: 15 full-time, 9 part-time
Statement of purpose. The owner of this small zoo has a need to keep track of his animals. He needs to know the genealogy for each animal and where it is caged currently in order to plan mating schedules.

 Case study 4: Household

Type of business: n/a
Employees: n/a
Statement of purpose. All you need to do is keep track of the total value for all your depreciable assets so you can give it to your accountant once a year.

Part 1
Preparing to design a database

1
CHAPTER

The elements of an application

You need to make a decision. You have decided to use your computer to help you make that decision. Furthermore, you have settled on a relational database software to manage the information and deliver it to you quickly and in a meaningful format. You might have even attempted to create a database with a table here and a table there. Now that approach is not giving you that vital decision-making information you need.

What an application is

You are ready to dig in. You want to get this new tool working for you as quickly as possible. What are the tasks ahead? How do you create the set of directions necessary to make the computer do what you need?

First, you must identify what kind of information you expect. What kind of information will help you make that decision? What related decisions do you need to make? What is the scope of the help that you envision? In effect, what are the requirements for your application?

An *application* is a customized use of database software intended to solve a business problem. An application can identify and formalize the elements involved in making decisions, and thus can provide a decision-maker with appropriate information of value relating to the available choices. Another application might simply be the means for storing and retrieving data stored in a database.

---

 application A customized use of database software intended to solve a specific business problem.

All applications, whether simple or complex, involve a translation from information to computer-based data and back to information, which is hopefully now of more value (Fig. 1-1). Information is input into the application, is manipulated or managed as application data, and is then output as information of value, or decision information. A "good" application could be defined as one that manages this input-output process efficiently and without error, thus enabling you to make decisions efficiently and without mistakes.

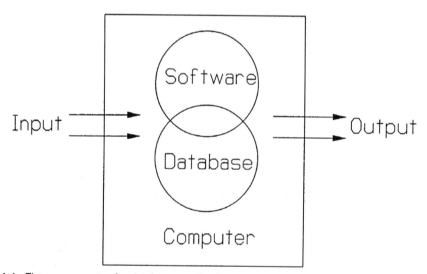

1-1 The components of a database application.

Database software that is used to implement or to install an application on a PC is often called *application-development software*. PC relational-database software is just one kind of application-development software. Relational-database software is used both to create the tables for data storage and also to manage the actual input and output from those tables.

---

 application-development software Database software used to implement or install an application on a PC.

4

You can look at the use of application-development software as having two phases—the *development* phase, during which you build the tables and design input and output mechanisms (loosely called *objects*) that the application will need to use, and the *implementation* phase, during which you actually work with real data. The implementation phase allows you to put the development to the test—to use the objects your design process has yielded.

Developing an application is something like building a bridge—you design it, you build it, and only then can you actually use it to get to the other side. Only once an application has been created is it ready to be used; only then can you begin to input and output your information.

Application development focuses first on database design, because the database is truly the foundation of any application. Everything depends on the database—how you input and output, what you can input and output, and even how easy it is to input and output. Perhaps most importantly, the quality of your output—how useful it is—depends on the database. As Fig. 1-2 suggests, your ability to make a decision depends directly on the effectiveness of the database design. If you have built a solid foundation—a database designed for maximum usefulness, com-

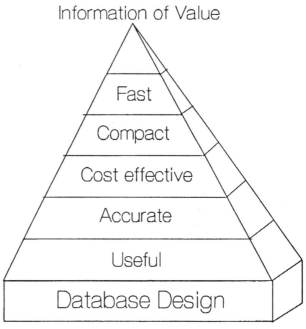

1-2 The database design pyramid provides information of value.

pactness, accuracy, speed, and cost effectiveness—how you get information in and out becomes a question of form rather than substance.

The process of database design, and the content of this book, thus focuses on the five issues mentioned above:

- Usefulness
- Compactness
- Accuracy
- Speed
- Cost effectiveness

A database is most useful if it is clearly focused on achieving a goal (chapter 2). A database is most compact if it follows relational standards to reduce redundancy (chapters 4, 5, and 6). A database is most accurate if it adheres to rules of integrity (chapter 7). A database is fastest if it is optimized for a specific environment (chapters 8 and 9), and a database is most cost effective if it is evaluated in the context of both costs and benefits (chapter 10).

Before getting into the details, it is important to understand the role the database software plays in all this. What actually is database software, and what is it intended to do?

What a Database Management System is

A database management system, or *DBMS*, is software that is designed to allow you to manage data of a wide variety of types. In this text, DBMS is used in both the singular (to represent a single database-management system) and the plural (to represent multiple database-management systems). Remember, you and your computer speak different languages, and software is intended to provide the translation. You can look at a DBMS as a software universe in which you create an application customized to meet your specific needs (see Fig. 1-3). A DBMS can give you access to a great wealth of information from a broad collection of data. However, to start, why are there two terms—information and data? What is the difference between the two, and why is the distinction important?

 DBMS (database management system)   Software designed to allow you to manage a wide variety of data types to meet a variety of needs.

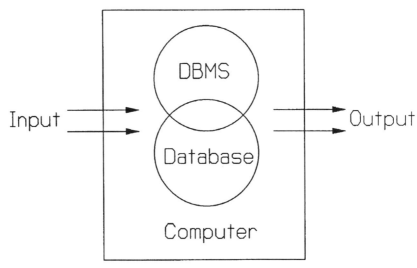

1-3 A database application under DBMS software.

Storing data and using information

Data is facts. The word data is actually the plural of datum, but is used commonly as a singular description of something known or assumed. Data is meaningless because it provides no organization or context. Figure 1-4 displays data elements, which might or might not be related in some way. A jumble of alphabetic characters on a page explains nothing; those same characters grouped into words with a certain structure suddenly become a meaningful poem. Words and numbers randomly appearing on a page probably tell you nothing useful; organized words and numbers are immediately recognizable as the names and addresses of specific people. Data when organized is known as *information*. Information is what you use in your business. Information is what is created when data elements strewn across a page are grouped into employee names, identifiers, and telephone numbers (Fig. 1-5).

---

 data   Facts (plural), or a fact (singular), meaningless because it lacks context.

 information   Organized data.

How a DBMS manages data

Like other software, a DBMS is intended to provide a translation between the information that you work with and the information that the computer

102   Bill   107   555-8765

555-6121

Cranston

555-1111

Johnson

110

103   Sharon

Humphrey   Julie

Matthews

Martha   234-4433

1-4 Data (unorganized).

102
Bill Johnson
234-4433

103
Martha Humphrey
555-8765

107
Sharon Cranston
555-6121

110
Julie Matthews
555-1111

1-5 Information (organized).

can keep track of. A DBMS is a *database* management system rather than an *information* base management system because all the information that you provide is translated into its component data elements by the DBMS. These data elements then can be stored, modified, manipulated, or extracted back into information that you use. The DBMS uses specific tools to perform each of these tasks.

Using a DBMS can be simple, much like making a sketch, filling in blanks on a form, or crossing an incorrect value off of a list. On the other hand, these "simple" tasks can be relatively hard to perform, and can require learning a whole language unique to the DBMS. Different DBMSs require you to have widely varying skills to get anything done. DBMSs that are easy to use are intuitive and help you learn and get things done at the same time. An easy-to-use DBMS tends to give you a lot of help through detailed menus with simple and well-defined choices, and screens that look something like (or sometimes a lot like) physical objects you are already familiar with.

 easy-to-use   A DBMS that is intuitive and provides lots of help through detailed menus and well-defined choices, with screens that look a lot like the physical objects you are already familiar with.

The relational DBMS difference

The definition of a relational database is based on the concept that everything about an application (e.g., all the data that is to be managed by the application) can be stored in tables. For the purpose of this preliminary discussion, a table is nothing more than a single set of rows and columns (see Fig. 1-6).

C.J. Date, one of the earliest contributors to relational-database theory, defines a relational database as "a database that is perceived by its users as a collection of tables (and nothing but tables)" (1990, 112). This concept is fundamental to a relational database because it allows for *data independence*, the isolation of data from the mechanisms the DBMS uses to access that data. When a system supports data independence, users of that system are not required to ever know how the data is stored or how to access it—only that it exists in some logical format (described more in detail below).

 data independence   A quality of data that describes the fact that it is accessible through a logical format, and whose users need never know how it is physically stored.

9

Column

Name	Height	Build
Mark	Tall	Muscular
Mark	Short	Thin
Margaret	Tall	Thin
Karen	Tall	Athletic
Diane	Short	Thin

Row

1-6 A table includes both rows and columns.

Other types of databases, including structured or hierarchical databases, also manage data in tables. However, nonrelational databases usually relate or link the data in different tables through a program. A *program* is nothing more than a set of directions you create and save that a DBMS then can follow once or many times. A relational database is by definition more flexible than other types of databases, because changes to a relational application often can be made by changing the data, not the program. Changes to data are easily made; changes to programs usually are not.

 program A set of directions you create and save that tell a DBMS what things to do and in what order.

Relational theory, initially developed by E.F. Codd in the late 1960s, is unique in that it applies mathematical logic to the realm of database management (Codd, 1970). In fact, the term *relational* is used in this context because of the theory's basis in relational algebra. The theory itself is a set of rules that define different aspects of the ideal relational DBMS. This idealized DBMS is known as the *relational model*. Originally, the model was defined by 12 basic rules, but over time it has been expanded and now encompasses over 300 rules (Codd, 1990).

relational model A set of rules based on relational algebra that describe data structures using mathematical principles. The model describes three aspects of database management: data structures, data integrity, and data manipulation. The data structures are intended to reduce redundancy in data storage, and also to provide efficiency, security, and integrity across databases that are both shared and integrated.

DBMS software that is advertised as "relational" is usually only relational to one degree or another—only to the extent that it follows the rules established by the theory (see chapter 8 for how to evaluate a specific DBMS). There currently is no commercially available software that follows all the rules, either for a PC or for any larger minicomputer or mainframe system. However, for the purposes of this book, a relational DBMS (sometimes called an RDBMS) is simply software that is *intended* to manage data stored in relational tables (see chapter 4 for more detail on relational tables).

 RDBMS (relational DBMS) DBMS software that (to one degree or another) follows the rules laid out by the relational model.

Most applications built with a relational-database-management system (even the simplest) rely on data encompassed within multiple tables. As suggested by Fig. 1-7, the data in these tables define actual objects and processes, while at the same time also defining the relationships between the tables.

What a DBMS does

DBMS functions can be divided into five basic categories (see Fig. 1-8). Every DBMS should allow you to:

- Create and modify data structures
- Add, modify, manipulate, or delete data
- Manage data security and integrity
- Customize data input and output
- Automate or enhance the use of the other features

Each DBMS differs in how these features are used, and even in which are specifically available. However, you should use these categories to help you understand what your DBMS is designed to do for you.

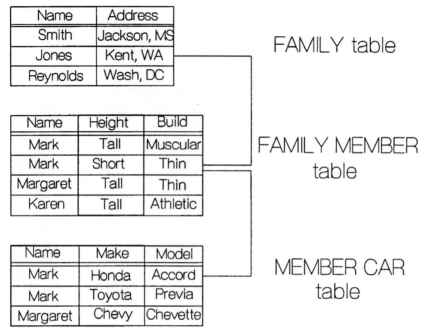

Name	Address
Smith	Jackson, MS
Jones	Kent, WA
Reynolds	Wash, DC

FAMILY table

Name	Height	Build
Mark	Tall	Muscular
Mark	Short	Thin
Margaret	Tall	Thin
Karen	Tall	Athletic

FAMILY MEMBER table

Name	Make	Model
Mark	Honda	Accord
Mark	Toyota	Previa
Margaret	Chevy	Chevette

MEMBER CAR table

1-7 A relational database.

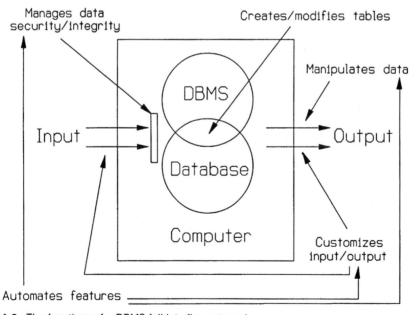

1-8 The functions of a DBMS fall into five categories.

Creating and modifying data structures

Most DBMSs allow you to work with data elements that can be extracted and manipulated independently of any other data elements. Unlike elements (words) in a word-processed document, DBMS data elements usually are not linked sequentially. Instead, they are stored within a separately defined database structure known as *tables*. The database structure is discussed in greater detail later in this chapter.

The tools for creating and modifying a database structure differ from DBMS to DBMS. However, most allow you to build a new structure (a table or tables), and to modify that structure once built.

Adding, modifying, manipulating, or deleting data

Once a table has been created, you can use a DBMS to enter data, make changes to data, or delete data. Most DBMSs also have powerful tools for manipulating, summarizing, and analyzing data. These capabilities allow you to perform calculations, combine data, and translate data directly to and from other DBMSs or related software.

Data manipulation also includes *data extraction*, or the capability to ask questions about the data. The DBMS feature that performs this type of task normally is called a *query*. It is worth noting that the speed with which a DBMS retrieves data through a query is one of the benchmarks used for judging a DBMS product. Querying is a crucial feature in any DBMS, because most applications rely heavily on queries as the basis for outputting information of value.

---

 query A technique for asking questions or doing analysis on data managed by a DBMS.

In a RDBMS, data-manipulation features ordinarily include the capability to handle multiple sets of data at the same time. A RDBMS usually can combine or separate data from more than one structure through a single operation.

Managing data security and integrity

Most DBMSs include the capability to control who can use the data structure and data-manipulation features described above. In addition, a DBMS might allow you to specify under what circumstances the use of such features is allowable. This kind of control is usually a critical aspect of your application. Without accurate and valid data, any information compiled by the application and provided as output to you will be unreliable, and thus useless as a tool for making a decision.

Data security describes the control the DBMS exerts over who can do what in an application. Security can be seen as a matrix that compares each user to each item of data. In its simplest form, data security defines data table by table, and each user's ability to access the data is specified through a yes or no (see Table 1-1). In reality, data security usually is enforced through a more complicated set of definitions that can identify specific data elements (not just tables) along with which of several types of access are allowable.

---

 data security   The control the DBMS exerts over who can do what in an application.

Table 1-1   The simplest kind of data security: is access allowed to the rows?

	User Mark	Steve	Judy
Family	Yes	Yes	Yes
Member	No	No	Yes
Member car	No	Yes	Yes

One of the reasons that data security is a primary concern in a business system is because without it the validity of the data can be compromised quickly. Even with appropriate security in effect, data entry and modification will always include inadvertent errors. Whenever possible, a DBMS should reduce the frequency of these kind of errors.

Data integrity describes the accuracy and validity of data in an application relative to the requirements of the business. As discussed in more detail below (and in chapter 2), the database design specifies what data you will keep track of and how that data is related. The design also specifies details about what makes the data being tracked correct—in other words, what you expect for each data element (see chapter 5). A DBMS should help make sure that these details are applied consistently, and thus that the data will be accurate. In other words, a value you think is a social security number is in the appropriate format, a date for a newly purchased item is within the current month and year, and an invoice number falls within allowable range of values. A DBMS also should help ensure that the data is valid, i.e., that a two-digit state abbreviation describes a real state, or that a department number represents a real department in the business system.

 data integrity The accuracy and validity of data in an application relative to the requirements of the business.

Customizing data input and output

In addition to the basic features necessary to maintain the data, most DBMSs provide a wide variety of features that enable you to control how you actually work with the data. These features allow you to control the organization and format of what you work with in order to help you use information, rather than merely data.

In effect, these features enable the translation from your information to and from data. Even if a query is used to compile the information, a report or graph or screen image actually will deliver it. The closer the appearance of that image is to the information you need, the more readily you will be able to derive information of value from it (and, not coincidentally, the easier the application will be to use).

This kind of organization and formatting is fundamentally different from the type of organization developed through a database design. As described in detail in chapter 2, the database design deals with relational logic applied to your data. Customized data input and output, on the other hand, address your need to deal with this data as information. Each different user of the data might (and probably will) have a different need for information. Even as a single user of your application, you will probably want to enter (input) or gather (output) different information from the system at different times. You might need to enter a new patient and his appointment time today, but tomorrow you might need to print a list of all the patients and their addresses. The next day you might want to print your appointments for next week. Each different need is associated with different information.

At one level, customization of data input and output involves identifying the information you need for a specific purpose. This kind of specification is called a *view* (see Fig. 1-9). In some DBMSs, views are created and modified in a way similar to tables. The only difference is that the elements of a view are not data elements themselves; views just identify where among the tables the actual data elements can be found.

 view A combination of fields from tables that acts like a table itself. A view normally is used for a specific input or output process.

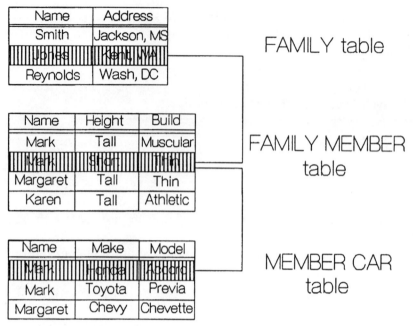

Name	Address
Smith	Jackson, MS
Jones	Kent, WA
Reynolds	Wash, DC

FAMILY table

Name	Height	Build
Mark	Tall	Muscular
Mark	Short	Thin
Margaret	Tall	Thin
Karen	Tall	Athletic

FAMILY MEMBER table

Name	Make	Model
Mark	Honda	Accord
Mark	Toyota	Previa
Margaret	Chevy	Chevette

MEMBER CAR table

1-9 A relational database combines data in multiple tables through combining specific rows of data.

At another level, customization of data input and output involves actually presenting the data in a view through a report, a graph, or simply on the computer screen. DBMS features in this category include *report designers*, which allow you to customize the output of the data as it appears in a written format. Graph designers also fall into this category. A *graph designer* allows you to create and customize the graphic display of your data, either to be printed out or to be shown on screen.

Many DBMSs include some kind of form generator as well. A *form* is an image on the computer screen that is used to access data, to input new data, or to look at or modify data that already has been input. A *form generator* is a DBMS tool used to build a form, and it works much like a report generator for output on the screen. A form usually specifies details such as the placement of the data on the screen, the order in which you enter or move through the data elements, and cosmetic details, such as the colors of different areas of the screen or what kind of borders will surround them.

 form An image on the computer screen that is used to access data; to input new data, or to look at or modify data that has already been input.

Automating or enhancing other features

The last category of DBMS features allow you to customize the way that your application works. Remember, the intent is to deliver information of value. You can see from the discussion of the other DBMS features that the delivery of this information might well be dependent upon not one, but several features of the DBMS.

Without help, you would be forced to go through several steps in order to get what you need. For example, to determine your schedule for today, you might need to build a query to select only those appointments for today, design a report to lay out each appointment against a grid of the available appointment times, and finally output that report to your printer or onto your screen.

However, most DBMSs support features that enable you to automate this kind of task. *Automation* involves creating a *program*, simple as it might be, that tells the DBMS what to do so you don't have to. Instead of going through each step every time you need a printed copy of your schedule, you perform one step, relying on the DBMS to follow through with the rest of the steps. Automating thus can be seen as creating a layer of control that customizes how the DBMS interacts with you (see Fig. 1-10). Automating allows you to use the DBMS to perform a task without your having to remember all the steps every time. Once you've created a menu structure (built the program), you can ignore the details of the steps, and making a simple choice can allow input, output, or some combination of both to occur.

This category of DBMS features is often called a *programming language* because it allows you to create and save the necessary instructions as a program. The DBMS will then follow these instructions each time you direct it to. DBMS programming tools are often the most difficult to understand and work with, because they are essentially similar to any other programming language, such as BASIC or PASCAL or C.

---

 programming language   Those features of the DBMS that allow you to automate or customize the use of the other features.

All the features of the DBMS should be used to accomplish the overall goal of the application: to deliver information of value to you. A DBMS programming language gives you the power to define what you need just once, and then rely on the DBMS to get it done.

However, how do you go about defining what you need? Specifically, what kinds of things does the DBMS have to do for you in order to deliv-

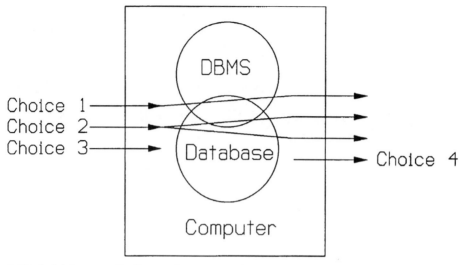

1-10 A database application can be automated to create one choice that performs several input/output tasks.

er information of value? Although you now should have a sense of what a DBMS is or should be able to do, it might not be so clear which of these features you need for your application. The features that will be important to you depend on what you need to accomplish, or more to the point, what you need the application to do.

What an application does

The things you need the DBMS to do usually are nothing more than inputs and outputs, and sometimes "internal" manipulations. These operations can be termed jointly *application tasks* (see Fig. 1-11).

---

 application tasks   Things you need the DBMS to do, usually involving input or output from the database.

Defining decision-oriented tasks   C.J. Date, along with other database theorists, draws a distinction between operational and decision support databases. *Operational databases*, according to Date, focus on "routine, highly repetitive applications . . . executed over and over again to support the day-to-day operation of the enterprise." *Decision-support databases* "frequently [consist] of summary information (e.g., totals, averages), where that summary information in turn is extracted from the operational database on a periodic basis—say once a day or once a week" (1990,

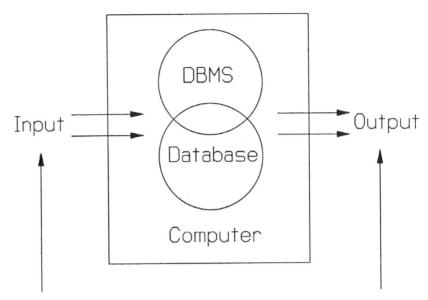

1-11 The input and output are application tasks.

10–11). In this sense, the tasks an operational database might be expected to perform would differ dramatically from those a decision-support database might. However, for the purposes of this discussion, both types of databases are assumed to be encompassed within a single, decision-oriented database. Practically speaking, most small to mid-size applications do combine both types of requirements into one. For example, you'll probably use just one application—one database—to both help you track current activity and predict upcoming activity.

An application normally includes the following decision-oriented tasks:

- Reports generated
- Graphs displayed
- Questions answered
- Analyses performed

These tasks are focused clearly on getting you information of value and basically define the output of the application (see Fig. 1-12).

Identifying maintenance tasks

In addition to the decision-oriented tasks, an application must support the maintenance of the data itself. Without the mechanisms in place to keep

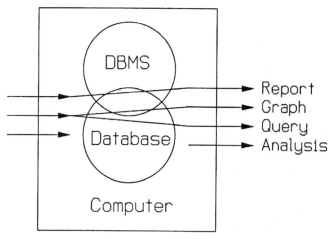

1-12 Automating application output.

the data up-to-date, any business system will quickly fail. The information will not be of value because it will be obsolete.

The data must be entered, edited where appropriate, and deleted when necessary. From your point of view, these tasks often are the most time-consuming in an application, and thus weigh heavily in any cost analysis (see chapter 10). Data input and maintenance can, however, be streamlined by taking advantage of different options supported by many DBMSs. In addition to entering data from the keyboard, many DBMSs support the entry of data through file import from other software, by moving data from one table to another within the database or from other physical sources, such as a scanner or a bar-code reader. These jointly define the input for the application (see Fig. 1-13).

In addition to those tasks specifically related to data maintenance, other tasks are necessary to support the application itself. These tasks usually include the development of backup and recovery procedures to protect against the time when the computer will fail. *Backup* refers to the process of making a copy (often in some kind of compressed mode) of the application programs and data (the output side). *Recovery* refers to the process of returning the application to its original state (the input side).

---

backup The process of making a copy of the application programs and data (often in some kind of compressed mode).

recovery The process of returning an application to a pre-failure state after a problem has occurred.

20

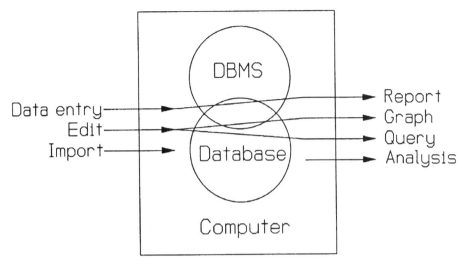

1-13 Automating application input and output.

Backup and recovery tasks all relate to the process of entering and maintaining data within the structures of the database.

What data structures are

All DBMSs manage data (see Fig. 1-14). Data managed by an RDBMS is always managed in tables. A table, in its simplest form nothing more than a set of rows and columns, is commonly used to keep information in an organized format. You have already encountered and intuitively understood tables in many contexts completely unrelated to databases, such as sports "box scores," tide tables, and questionnaires.

An RDBMS table is a lot like these other kinds of tables. However, a *relational table* (the data structure used by an RDBMS) is unique in several important ways. In fact, a relational table differs enough from what people commonly regard as a table that the relational model uses different terms entirely to describe it such as relations, or R-tables (see chapter 4 for a more detailed discussion of relations). However, in this book I use the more familiar term "table" when referring to a relational table.

A *table* consists of a grid of rows and columns and looks a lot like a simple spreadsheet. Each row contains data, all of which relate to a single object or process. Each column contains data that describe one attribute of that object or process (see Fig. 1-15).

For example, data about members of your family could be stored in a

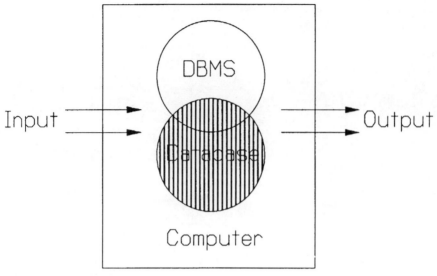

1-14 The database component of an application.

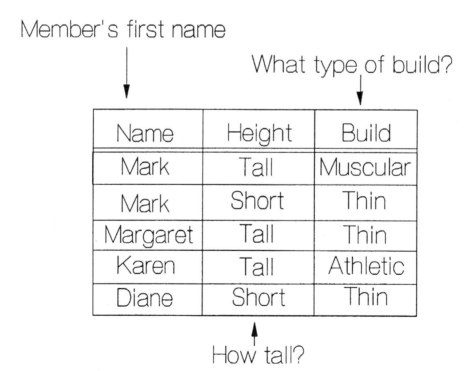

1-15 The columns in a table.

table that listed each member's name, height, and build. Each family member's data would be represented by a single row, and each type of stored data would be represented within a single column, i.e., "Name," "Height," or "Build."

---

 relation   A special kind of table that has been modified to follow the rules of the relational model.

Working with logical tables

For the purpose of simplicity, thus far the term *table* has been used to describe the way a DBMS, and specifically an RDBMS, manages and stores data. In fact, there is a big difference between the concept of a table and the way data actually is stored by the DBMS on a disk storage device (a hard or floppy disk).

The terms *logical table* and *physical table* describe these two different ways of understanding the way a DBMS manages data. A table (as this book uses the term) is more specifically a logical table, because it is really just a disciplined way of thinking about how the data is stored. Each DBMS manages the physical storage of the data in its own way. Thus, a single logical table could be stored in many different physical table formats. To you, or any other user of the DBMS, the data will look the same, regardless of the particular physical table format being used. This follows directly from the data independence achieved by the relational model; you can ignore the physical format as long as the integrity of the logical tables is preserved (see Fig. 1-16).

---

 logical table   A table that is conceived by application users to think about and manipulate data.

Understanding physical tables

Some DBMSs translate each table into an individual file. Some DBMSs combine all tables in a given database into a single file. Some DBMSs combine table data and all associated DBMS activities regarding that data into a related group of files.

---

 physical table   The organization for data as it is stored.

This separation between logical and physical tables sometimes is

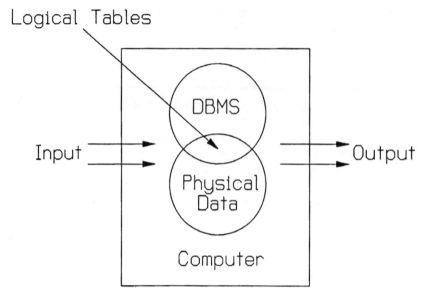

1-16 Logical tables are used by the DBMS and users to conceptualize the physical storage of the data.

described in slightly different terms. A physical table can be considered part of an *internal level* or *storage view* that is concerned primarily with the way the data is stored on the disk; a logical table is sometimes regarded as existing on a conceptual level. In other words, a logical table consists of all the tables and their relationships; a third level, known as the *external level*, is used sometimes to describe the way individual users access the data, roughly equivalent in scope to the definition of a view given earlier in this chapter (Tsichritzis and Klug, 1978).

Regardless of terminology, the physical structure of the data is one feature that differentiates one DBMS from another. Many RDBMSs use proprietary structures that cannot be accessed by any other software. Data from this kind of RDBMS must be translated in order to be usable by any other kind of DBMS, or by any other kind of software. A translation of this kind often is called *exporting* (my software to yours) or *importing* (your software to mine).

---

 export   A translation of data from your DBMS to the format of another software program.

 import   A translation of data from another software program into your DBMS.

Some RDBMSs use a more standard structure, with data stored in physical files with the *DBF* (database file) extension. This specific kind of file name describes a (debatably) nonproprietary type of physical data structure. The class of DBMS known as XBase products utilize this rather generic form of physical storage. DBF data structures are accessible directly by a variety of DBMS products.

Again, an RDBMS that supports data independence should allow the physical structure of the data to be of little importance to you. After all, it is the RDBMS's job to act as the interpreter between the computer and you; translating data between the physical and logical realms is a perfect example of this interpretive kind of task.

To review briefly, a relational DBMS manages data in tables. A table is thus the only kind of RDBMS data structure. If no other qualifier is used, in this book the term *table* refers to a *logical, relational* table.

Remember, the DBMS controls the application. It both manages the data in the tables and allows the input and output to occur. However, even the most highly automated application will still rely on you to make it work. After the design process is over, you must still play a role, but what role is that? What kinds of things should you expect to contribute to ensure your application's success?

Using an application

Any functioning application involves a combination of human and automated resources. Even those tasks that are managed clearly by the computer depend, to a greater or lesser degree, on the people who interact with it. The automated part of the business system depends on the people to gather the necessary information, to convey this information to the computer in some way, and to demand information in return.

The people who work with an application fall into two categories: those who support the maintenance of the data (the gathering and conveying, or input), and those who rely on the data to make decisions (the demanding, or output). Both categories of people can be considered system users. In a smaller system, most users assume both roles. In a larger system, management-level people usually have little responsibility for day-to-day data maintenance, while staff workers have little need for decision-oriented information.

---

 user   A person who works with an application, either to maintain the data or to rely on it, to aid in the decision-making process.

In a small business system, the application developer also might be the focus for the delivery of the information of value. Obviously, you're your own designer here. Depending on the degree of automation (sometimes called *sophistication*) of your application, obtaining input and output might be very simple or very complicated, either fast or very slow. Don't confuse sophistication with complexity; the most sophisticated applications are often deceptively simple to use.

---

sophistication   The degree of automation of an application that makes use of the system as easy as possible.

An application that meets its goal will allow a user to demand, and to obtain, information of value. However, in order for that to happen, the application must be maintained. Any system, computer-based or not, requires monitoring on an ongoing basis. Data that is input must be kept up to date, work in process must be copied (*backed-up*) in case of system failure, and useless or out-of-date data must be archived or removed. These tasks and others like them are called *system maintenance*, and they can occupy a substantial portion of the time required to make the system work. If your application is used by more than one individual, these tasks likely will occupy an even greater amount of time.

---

maintenance   The ongoing work done to an application that is required in order to ensure that it continues to work.

Summary

In this chapter, you encountered some basic concepts that should help you understand the foundation of any database management system. Specifically, you learned that:

- Data and information are not the same. You work with information while a computer deals with data.

- A Database Management System, or DBMS, stores and manipulates data of many kinds to provide you with a wide range of information.

- An application usually involves tasks directed toward decision-assistance (delivering information of value), but also must involve data input and maintenance tasks.

- *Data storage* describes the way a computer keeps track of the data, while *input* and *output* involve how you move data in and out.
- A DBMS usually stores data in tables consisting of rows and columns.
- You and all other users are integral to the success of your business system.

2
CHAPTER

The database design process

You've taken a look at the boundaries of what an application can do. This perspective is certainly interesting and very helpful in concept, but what about your needs? How does all this relate to what you want to get done?

Now is the time to start getting specific. You need to be able to imagine what your own application will look like. You need to begin creating an application design—to draft the blueprint for your application, but understanding the components of a generic application isn't enough, it doesn't really equip you to begin the process of creating your own.

What you need is a methodology for application design. A methodology in this sense is nothing more than a series of steps that you can follow. At this point you need to understand the process as well as the result.

Developing an application

You might imagine that application development is a straight-line process. Follow step one, step two, and step three, and you'll arrive at a point where your application is complete. This assumes that the application is a product, a result of the development process.

Let's take a closer look at the definition of a application. As defined in chapter 1, an *application* is a customized use of database software intended to solve a business problem. Because an application is a product, application development follows the classic cycle. The *life cycle* is so called because it spans the life of the business system, from beginning to end (see Fig. 2-1).

life cycle A development process that spans the life of the system being developed and usually encompasses steps from the identification of the requirements through the installation, training, and evaluation of the system.

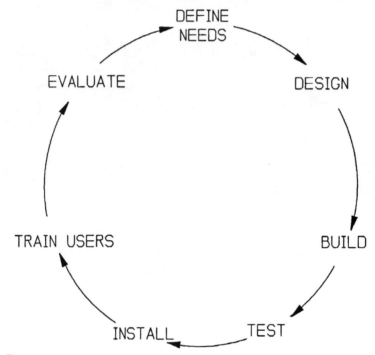

2-1 The application-development life cycle.

In many ways, application development is not a true cycle. It begins with the conceptualization of the target: the end result, or what the system will do. From that point on, the development proceeds through the design, building, and testing of the application, installation and training, and evaluation of the implemented system. Evaluation usually happens naturally, as people complain about problems: invalid results, slow processes, awkward tasks. The evaluation thus leads to a redefinition of the requirements, which starts the cycle again. However, now the requirements are closer to the end result, and thus the cycle should take less time. Note that this quickening development cycle only really applies in a relational database system. It is, in fact, part of the power of a relational system that it is flexible enough to allow for redesign—in fact, to encourage it. Nonrelational systems are so rigid that redesign often involves as much time as designing the first time around.

In practice, a life cycle can continue indefinitely. A final end result, so carefully evaluated and planned for, is often unreachable. This could be true for several reasons. First, once an application is implemented, the end result (the target) is bound to change. It is always much easier to conceptualize an end result when you have pieces of it already available than when everything is still on paper. Second, the requirements for a system could become obsolete before the system is even implemented. The computer industry is changing so quickly that the cost/benefit to making a different hardware selection or integrating several applications can justify a substantial change in the requirements. Third, the development could end prematurely because the benefit to be had in continuing to make modifications just doesn't justify the cost. In effect, the application might not be ideal, but it works.

You might find this kind of process unsatisfying, or even unacceptable. It certainly isn't mathematically pure, in the sense that A (identified end result) plus B (application development process) always equals C (ideal application). The process of building an application is not now, nor will it ever be, an exact science, because what you are trying to do is translate human thought into computer processing. The languages are different, and thus the translation will never be exact.

This isn't an insurmountable problem; it shouldn't scare you to think that you are shooting at a target you'll never hit. The process has its own benefits. First, you'll probably discover things about your business that you never had time to contemplate before. Second, you might be surprised to uncover better ways of doing business, even for those tasks that aren't computer-based. Finally, even a rough-and-ready application is likely to prove invaluable.

The database design step in system design

As mentioned earlier, database design is only one component of the application development phase. This is because the database is only one component of the application itself, albeit the most important one. This book is not intended to cover the entire scope of application design, but just as a matter of perspective, application design should include the following:

- The specifics of hardware (what kind of computer(s) will be used)
- Operating system(s)

- Software (DBMS and other)
- Communications (within the same business system or between business systems, locally or over a distance)
- Integration (controlling relationships between different hardware, software, operating system, and communications elements).

The human components of the business-system design include the specifics of who will use the system and for what purpose, how those users will relate to one another, who will be responsible for what area of the business system, and what kind of training will be required initially and in the long-term for those users.

The development of the database design will need to take some of the above elements into consideration. The hardware/software components that are proposed will have a large impact on the type of database design used. For the purposes of this book, the business system design is assumed to include implementation on a PC-based system (either with one or multiple users), using a RDBMS.

Input and output will need to be identified in order for you to decide appropriately what type of data will need to be managed by the RDBMS. However, you can't make those assessments until you've taken a closer look at database design.

What a database design is

A database design is an object: an actual, physical document that describes in textual and graphic detail the data structures required for a given business system. The term *object* is used by this industry in a very specific way (to describe the software analog of a real world thing) (Mullin 1989). The usage here does not relate to that definition; "object" here is used simply to describe a material thing that occupies space. These structures include both a definition of the logical tables and a description of the boundaries of the data to be found within those tables. In many ways, a database design is a model of the data itself. The model must be very detailed, detailed enough that the entire application can be built confidently on this foundation. However, the model also should be real enough so that you can describe it without special terminology, and straightforward enough so that you can summarize it on a single piece of paper.

Don't be misled—database design is still a part of application design cycle. The design will be modified and enhanced and tweaked. Simply regard the first cycle as being highly dependent on the quality of the database design. If you do a good job with the "first time" design, you're starting out on a firm foundation.

An overview of the database design process

The process of database design begins with a concept of the overall application. The application should be able to take what you know and translate it into what the computer can handle. "What you know" in this situation relates not only to the information you work with, but also to the work flow that you live every day, the process of doing business.

The database design process starts with a firm grounding in relational theory, and then when necessary, moves to optimize the design (see Fig. 2-2). You start by defining the input/output, designing the tables, and identifying the integrity constraints on the data, but you could discover that this initial design doesn't meet your requirements from a performance or cost standpoint. Thus, after you apply a dose of reality, you'll most likely revisit those initial definitions. The theoretical side of the process is completely independent of any hardware or database product specifications, while reality remains oblivious to any restrictions of relational database modelling.

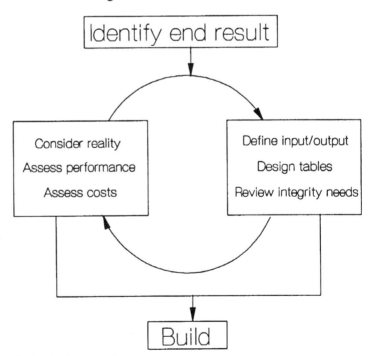

2-2 Steps in the database design process.

The first time around the theoretical design is addressed first. Once it is complete, the process continues with the consideration of the practical aspects of the design's implementation. Different RDBMS products have different requirements that will immediately have an impact on the design. Specifically, the degree to which the chosen DBMS conforms (or doesn't conform) to the relational model has a powerful effect on the design itself (see chapter 8). *Performance issues*, which address how fast different aspects of the implemented system must happen, also should be considered (see chapter 9). In addition, the costs of the system must be evaluated continually, because design decisions will have a major impact on the long-term cost of any business system (see chapter 10).

Identifying the end result

Any business solution must be preceded by a specific, identifiable need. If you can't express the requirement, you surely won't be able to concep-tualize a solution. The first step in the process of designing an application thus involves identifying the need. The output of an up-and-running appli-cation intended to meet this need could be called the *end result*—the tar-get in the life cycle.

Your end result is nothing more than a summary of what you want your application to do. You should be able to summarize your end result in a single, simple sentence. In a decision-oriented application, the end result normally will involve the delivery of information of value—an output.

---

 end result The output of an up-and-running application, and the goal of the application-development process.

To figure out your end result, ask two very specific questions: What do I need to know that this system will tell me? What will this informa-tion allow me to do? Table 2-1 asks and answers these questions for each of the case studies. Note that three out of the four cases specify the man-agement of a given business function as a goal for the application.

The application should be there to help the job get done. In a very real way, the end result of your application might well be parallel to the end result of your job. Asking the question "What do I do?" could lead directly to the answer, "What must my system help me do?" Even if you don't need a system to support you in every area of your job, under-standing the scope of what your job entails often will help put the requirements for your application in perspective. This perspective is essential in looking at the cost versus benefit equation examined in some detail in chapter 10.

Table 2-1 Case-study end results.

	Need to know	Need to do
🖥	Who is scheduled when	Manage time
💰	Who ordered what	Manage purchase orders
🐂	Which animals should be mated	Find mates
🏠	How much assets are worth	Keep list of assets

Table 2-2 lists some additional examples of end results. You'll note that many of these examples, like the case studies, include the term "management". *Management* is a term used frequently in regard to applications, for the same reason that it is a term used frequently to describe job responsibilities. In an application, *information management* usually spans the spectrum of DBMS tasks, including the input, processing and maintenance of the data, as well as the development of the required output, just as your job might span a similar spectrum of responsibilities.

Table 2-2 Database design end results.

Management of inventory
Archiving sales orders
Management of patient information
Management of employee information
Tracking attorney work flow
Management of vendor relationships
Management of daily tasks

Considering growth

You need to evaluate potential changes in your business when developing an application design. If growth is planned, or especially if rapid growth is likely, you should design to include future requirements as well as those for today. If your business has gone through the process of building a two-year or five-year business plan, growth projections could be as available as that document. However, if you haven't developed a written plan, this is a good time to take a look at this issue. A business plan is critical to the success of a business, and is at least as important to the success of a business system. If you're just starting out, there are many valuable references to assist you in the process of building a business plan, including pamphlets published by the Small Business Administration and many state business-assistance agencies.

Growth can impact several areas of an application, including:

- Number of users
- Speed of access to data
- Data storage requirements
- Data summaries

The users

As your business grows, so can the number of employees. More employees usually means more, and different, users for an application. If your system is designed for a single user, changing it to allow for multiple users can be a very painful process. This pain will arrive in the financial area; the costs associated with a multi-user system are substantially greater than those for a single user (see chapter 10). However, it will arrive also in the management-and-coordination area. For example, you might have designed a database with unique names that only you understand. Training another user to your naming conventions could be nearly impossible.

More generally, you might not have considered security issues in the design, and adding another user could involve creating password or other protection features to isolate sensitive information to or from the appropriate user(s). The issue of security often is addressed naturally at the point you have to install a multi-user system (a local-area network or larger). A *local-area network*, (also called a *LAN*), is simply a group of computers physically linked together with cables. Most LANs have PCs linked together, while some also link Macintosh, minicomputers, or other kinds of terminals together with PCs as well.

 LAN (local-area network) A group of computers physically linked together with cables, usually utilizing a special operating system to manage the interactions of the multiple users.

When evaluating your initial investment, you might have considered yourself the only potential user. This could have led you to decide to keep your investment in consultants or other programmers to a minimum. You might have planned to rely on your own skill to perform any computer-related tasks. Once other users are added, however, you might find that they don't have your competence nor your inclination toward supporting a computer-based system. This fact could wreak havoc in a loosely structured application that depends heavily on a well-trained user, in which the program doesn't provide a lot of help at getting things done. Table 2-3 describes the potential user-oriented difficulties encountered by the growth anticipated by RTS.

Table 2-3 RTS problems in personnel growth.

Current user plan:

RTS intends to do all the system maintenance himself. He will be inputting the required data and preparing all the reports. He intends to use the system at least two hours per day. RTS wants this system to be the foundation for all his work products, as well as provide him with a simple way to prepare bills using his verified schedule.

Growth expected:

Plans to double his client base within two years.

Problems anticipated:

Unable to manage the business on a one-man basis. Business system must be expanded to include at least one additional user (employee or partner).

Solutions explored:

Focus on application development that will make the business system as easy to use as possible, so when new users must be added, training time is minimized.

Consider making application easily modified from single- to multi-user.

Even an application initially designed for multiple users can be impacted dramatically by growth. Most multi-user systems have a limit to the number of users that they can support. This limit can be enforced through the hardware or software, i.e., no more than 50 users for a particular type of file server or no more than five users per purchase of a DBMS. More frequently a practical limit is reached through the degradation of performance (speed) when the number of users approaches some critical point. *Degradation of performance* is nothing more than the application slowing down. At some point, slowness will cause a system to fail, because users will elect not to use the system.

 performance The speed of an application measured against the application's requirements.

Speed

The speed of the different components of your application must be a factor in designing it. Even though speed is often difficult to assess, and particularly so when you are implementing an application for the first time, this evaluation is extremely important to the success of the system. An application that takes five seconds to react when you enter a keystroke, a report that takes overnight to print, or a query that takes three hours to process can cause a user to elect not to use the system.

Many issues impact the speed of a system, including the number of system users and the amount of data stored by a system. Chapter 9 takes a more detailed look at speed and directly addresses the issue of when you should modify a database design to maximize performance. Table 2-4 identifies the issues to be considered by EB, whose growth as planned will dramatically impact the speed requirements.

Table 2-4 EB growth problems.

Current user plan:

EB will name a single system administrator who will have primary responsibility for the maintenance of the multi-user network, as well as for the routine system maintenance chores. Each of the ten other group members will be required to utilize the system on a daily basis in order to input newly received requests, process purchase orders, and answer questions from vendors and users.

Growth expected:

Overall company has doubled its number of retail stores in the past 18 months and plans to continue this growth rate for the next two years (again doubling the number of stores).

Problems anticipated:

Purchasing activity must be able to keep pace with the additional demands of the new stores. Hiring freeze in nonmerchandise related activities means that the current users must be equipped to handle the growth. The purchasing system must be efficient (and fast) enough to allow each group member (buyer) to increase productivity to keep pace with the growth for a minimum of two years.

Solutions explored:

Focus on design issues that will maximize performance. Consider *batching* (processing only once per day or less frequently) certain noncritical activities to allow essential transactions to occur without interruption.

Investigate hardware upgrades to assist in speeding up processing tasks.

Put in place procedural mechanisms to ensure any available software upgrades are implemented immediately.

Consider phasing in additional system development that will reduce each user's impact on the other users.

Data storage requirements

The data stored by an application should reflect the business being done. The more business transactions that occur, the more data usually will be generated, and thus the more data will need to be stored. Business growth can involve increased numbers of clients, increased numbers of jobs for clients, increased numbers of patients, or increased numbers of sales, all of which will result in the need for greater data storage.

Business growth also could be reflected in the need for storing additional types of data. If all your clients are in a single industry, categorizing them is unimportant. If your business grows to encompass several industries, keeping track of which client is in which industry likely will become important.

Estimating the size of the data storage required can be a challenge, but it is important to the database design process. Generally speaking, when the volume of data to be stored is high, the importance of the relational model is proportionally high. A system task performed on one big table might work okay when there isn't very much data to be evaluated; the same task attempted when that table is very large could take a very long time, or could even cause the computer to lock up (an expression describing what often happens when the computer doesn't have enough resources, such as memory or disk storage, to complete a task). The amount of data stored has a strong impact on both the speed and efficiency of a application (see chapter 10 for more details).

Data is stored on a part of the computer called a *storage disk,* and both the size of the storage disk and the amount of data stored is measured in bytes. One *byte* is roughly equivalent to a single character of data. For example, the word "margarine" would take approximately nine bytes to be stored.

Originally, PCs had only floppy disk drives, and all data had to be stored on floppy diskettes. Older floppy diskette can hold 360,000 (360k) bytes of data. Today, high-density diskettes can hold up to 1,200,000 bytes (1.2 megabytes) of data. Smaller, better protected diskettes are also standard today, such as the newer, 3½-inch diskette, which comes built into its own case and can hold up to 1.44 megabytes of data.

Data on almost all PCs today is stored on a *hard disk drive* that is often internal (inside) the computer itself. This disk often is mounted permanently and can hold 20, 40, 80, 100, 200, or more megabytes of data. Newer technologies for disk storage involve laser disks (like the CD you use to listen to music) and optical disks. These kinds of disks usually can store much larger volumes of data than standard magnetic disks (which all the previously described types of disks are).

One of the advantages of a LAN is that it allows multiple users to have access to data stored in a central location on the LAN (often called a *file server*). Thus, the data storage used by an application can be a combination of data stored at individual PCs and data stored at a central location (or locations). In this scenario, an increase in the amount of data stored can be handled at one rather than many locations if this is desired.

It is difficult, if not impossible, to make even a rough assessment of the volume of data the system will need to store at the time you begin your database design. However, as the database design process continues, you should be aware that data storage is an issue. Be prepared to take a closer look at your data-storage requirements when the table designs are complete (see chapter 8).

Depth of detail

As the volume of data increases, so does the need to summarize that data. Reports that display the data in all its detail become more and more difficult to evaluate. The organization, combination, and analysis of data become a higher priority. In fact, the computer's facility at summarizing data is often a driving factor in developing an application in the first place.

In many cases, more data also leads to a need for graphic representation of data. Graphs display summarized data in a format that is more easily interpreted than a detailed report. Task specifications that include detail-level reports might need to be modified to include summarized reports and graphs.

To summarize, potential changes in the volume or types of data to be stored should be evaluated when beginning the design. If rapid growth is likely, you should design for future requirements wherever possible.

How to begin the design process

Once you have identified the end result and addressed some of the growth issues, now is the time to start breaking what you know down into manageable chunks. You must begin to organize your information in a way that can be used logically to describe that information. Remember that your design eventually will be implemented using the features of your RDBMS.

Now that you've done all this preparatory thinking, you're ready to sit down and begin the design. Your ideas might not flow easily, or they might not have any logic to them at first. However, there are a couple of tips that you can use to get started, and can help you maintain continuity once you've begun.

Sketching concepts on paper

A sketch is by far the easiest way to describe information about a database design. Remember, the design itself will end up in both written and graphic form; both formats can and should originate from rough sketches.

You might feel that designing a simple database is a straightforward exercise. You could whiz through the table and field designs, briefly pause at the development of table relationships, and be ready to create the structures within your chosen database within moments of opening your newly purchased DBMS.

However, you should be aware that even the simplest of designs will benefit from a sketch. Remember, the database design process isn't even computer-based until after the design is complete. You might want to turn your system on and get going, but your solution no doubt will be a short-lived one.

If you are concerned that your database design will be complex, a sketch is a first step toward providing simplicity. Even the most complex data and relationships can be described with a simple sketch. Even if you over-simplify, you can use a sketch to establish the boundaries for the different components of your application. Figures 2-3 through 2-6 illustrate preliminary sketches for each of the case-study applications.

Brainstorming

Throughout the process of creating your database design, assessment of the widest variety of possibilities is crucial. At this early point, the possi-

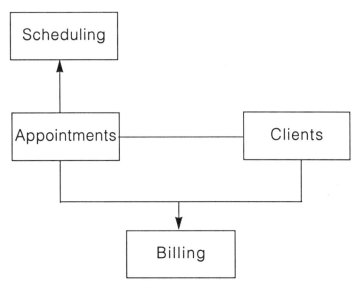

2-3 Sketch of the RTS database.

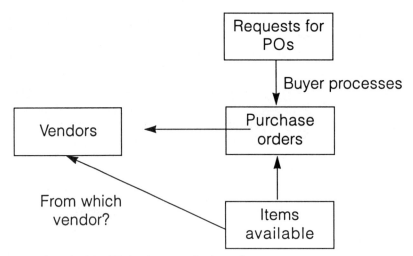

2-4 Sketch of the EB database application. 🐘

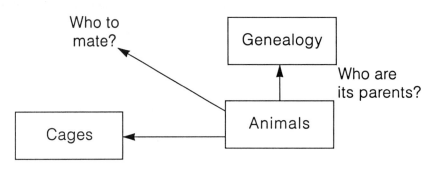

2-5 Sketch of the MH database application. 🐘

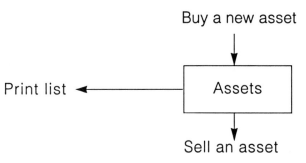

2-6 Sketch of the Asset Manager application. 🏠

bilities might only include problems to be solved, but within each problem identified early on lies the seed of its later solution.

Brainstorming is a proven method for provoking new and creative ideas. Taking the time to brainstorm might be difficult, but whatever time you can lend to the process up-front will only be of benefit. Even with limited time, devoting a few minutes to brainstorming with a pencil in hand should be a high priority.

Consider for a moment what other long term goals this application could meet. Does my business plan depend on application development for its success, and if so, what can I do to ensure that it happens? Is there any way to integrate more of my job into the application design? Are there tasks unrelated to my end result that might benefit from being computerized? Do I want to spend more time at the computer, or is my intention to use the application to free me from that kind of drudgery? Is there anyone in my group or professional contacts who might be willing to act as a sounding board for my database design?

These kinds of questions should help you keep an open mind as you progress through the database design process. You might discover that although there can be more than one right answer, or even several potential database designs that meet your basic requirements, the best solution might not be the most obvious one. Unless you allow yourself to explore alternative ways of thinking, you might never discover that less obvious, but better, solution. "Better" in this case refers to the degree to which the application meets the goal established by the end result.

Documenting the design process

Throughout the process of developing the details of your database design, be prepared to record them on paper. Simple sketches and notes from your brainstorming are really all that is necessary.

Recording your design as it evolves helps the process in two ways. First, taking the notes can help you think. The activities of drawing and writing often will provoke unique thoughts or unexpected solutions.

Second, having a written record of your thoughts and plans, even in the earliest stages, will prove invaluable. These notes and diagrams, rough as they might be, will become the basis for system documentation. *System documentation* is the written-in-English, published version of what the system does. System documentation can include two parts: *user documentation*, which details what the system does from a user's perspective, and *program documentation*, which explains how the code (any programmed part of the system) works.

system documentation   The written-in-English, published version of what the system does, usually including details from the user's perspective as well as from the programmer's perspective.

One of the most difficult parts of any system to document is its goals. Having the details of its development in writing will aid you or anyone to whom you delegate the task. Documenting the process as it occurs is valuable from a historical standpoint as well. Your design might be very broad to begin with, but could narrow as you continue the design process. If the system ever needs redesigning because of growth or migration to another type of system, the design documents will help provide a blueprint for evaluating the necessary enhancements or translations.

Creating a one-page database design diagram

You should keep in mind that one of the goals of the database design process is to develop a straightforward way to communicate the design. This is accomplished normally through the development of a single-page diagram that lays out the various tables in the design, the relationships between the tables, and any pertinent restrictions on the data. The critical areas of the completed system should be obvious on the sketch.

One sign that there is a problem with a database design is that the design cannot fit onto a single page. You should be sure to keep your design sketches close at hand. If at any point the overall sketch becomes too complex, reduce its complexity: summarize it. Figure 2-7 provides an

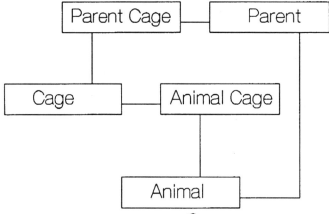

2-7 Intermediate database design sketch.

example of a single-page preliminary database design (early in the design process). If you get stumped along the way, take a look at the appendix to see where each of the case study designs will be ending up.

Defining the requirements

The database design will need to address two specific components of the application design:

- Input
- Output

The inputs and outputs for an application are crucial to the design of the database because they form the foundation for identifying the data that needs to be maintained. If an output is required, it needs data in order to occur, and the database design must take this fact into consideration. In fact, the process of designing the database begins here because it is much easier to remember inputs and outputs than it is to conceive of data elements in a vacuum. Remember, you deal with information while you work, and that information that you depend on must be available in the computer—in the database that you are designing. A complete business-system design would require an evaluation of the specific mechanisms for accomplishing these tasks, including the user skills and DBMS programming required, if any.

Table 2-5 describes a variety of tasks (inputs and outputs) that an application might be expected to accomplish. In developing your database design, it can be useful to lay out the tasks in a matrix like that in Table 2-5. The questions at hand are: who will do what, and how often will they need to do it? To make this kind of assessment for your application, you must first identify the tasks involved.

Table 2-5 Task/user matrix with expected frequency of performance.

Task	Manager	User 1	User 2
Print report		Daily	
Display graph	Weekly		
Print graph		Weekly	
Ask questions	Daily		Monthly
Do analysis	Daily	Weekly	Monthly
Input data		Daily	Daily
Modify data		Daily	

Identifying the input and output

The system tasks are the input and output required to support the application. As suggested by the Table 2-5 matrix, a list of tasks normally includes the following:

- Reports to be generated
- Graphs to be developed and displayed
- Questions to be answered
- Analyses to be performed
- Data to be input and maintained

Table 2-6 identifies the tasks for each of the case studies.

Table 2-6   Case-study tasks.

RTS needs to:

- Print a daily/weekly/monthly schedule
- Print invoices for clients
- Display a daily schedule on screen
- Display client information on screen
- Enter new appointments
- Modify the appointment schedule
- Enter client contacts
- Update client information

EB needs to:

- Print a list of purchase orders by user or item category
- Print a list of vendors
- Print an analysis of processing time by buyer
- Enter new purchase requests
- Modify current purchase requests
- Create purchase orders
- Close purchase orders
- Display purchase orders by user, vendor, or order date
- Maintain vendor, item and buyer data

MH needs to:

- Print a list of animals
- Print a genealogy for each animal
- Print a list of available cage space
- Enter new births
- Modify animal records
- Display all available data about an animal
- Maintain cage data

oops! Not using the system to accomplish the end result: identify appropriate mates. A well-designed system is not only able to store data but to analyze it as well. Not to utilize that capability dramatically reduces the effectiveness of the system.

You need to:

- Print a list of assets and depreciated values
- Enter newly purchased assets
- Delete assets that have been sold

Identifying the users and their tasks

Before you can identify which tasks will or should be performed by the user(s), it is important to take a look at who the user(s) are. Remember, users can fall into two categories: those who maintain the data, and those who use the data. Some users could, of course, do both. Table 2-7 identifies the users of each of the case study systems, while Table 2-8 identifies the task/user matrix for each of the case studies.

Table 2-7 Users of the case-study systems.

RTS is currently the sole user of the system.

EB will name a single system administrator who will have primary responsibility for maintenance of the multi-user network as well as other system-wide maintenance chores. There are 12 other users, of whom six are buyers who maintain their own relationships with vendors, with four being data entry personnel. The last two, the department head and the Vice President in charge of the department, will do no data maintenance but will be using the output generated by the business system to aid in decision-making.

MH will be the manager of the system. He intends to use two of his part-time staff to input the data when the system is set up and one of this staff to print reports once the system is up and running. He expects to use this part-time help only once a month, when he needs to generate the reports. His staff will notify him about births as they occur, and he will update the data himself.

You will be the sole user of the system.

Pay special attention to the mistake icon in Table 2-6. The most common problem encountered when evaluating the users and tasks associated with an application lies in underestimating the time it will take to manage the system. Even if MH believes that he will be able to make the time to support a new system, this is extremely unlikely, especially considering that he is not replacing a manual system with his new application. In his case, all these tasks are new and will take time away from his current job responsibilities. Unless he had time to spare before system implementation, he will be putting himself immediately in a situation that will lead quickly to application failure: lack of maintenance time.

Table 2-8 Case-study task/user matrix.

RTS is the sole user of the system, so each task will be performed by him.

Task	Frequency
Print a daily/weekly/monthly schedule	Daily
Print invoices for clients	Monthly
Display a daily schedule on screen	Daily
Display client information on screen	Daily
Enter new appointments	Daily
Modify the appointment schedule	Daily
Enter client contacts	Daily
Update client information	Weekly

EB

Task	System Admin	Buyers	DE Staff	Dept. Head	VP
Print PO list by user/item	Weekly				
Print vendors list	Weekly			Weekly	
Print process time analysis by buyer				Weekly	Weekly
Enter new requests			Daily		
Modify current purchase requests		Daily			
Create PO		Daily			
Close PO	Daily	Daily			
Display POs by user/vendor/date		Daily			
Maintain vendor/ item/buyer data			Daily		

MH

Task	MH	DE Help	Report Help
Print a list of animals			Weekly
Print a genealogy for each animal	Monthly		
Print a list of available cage space			Daily
Enter new births	Daily	(start-up)	
Modify animal records	Weekly	(start-up)	
Display all available data about an animal	Weekly		
Maintain cage data	As needed		

You will be the sole user of the system. You need to:

Task	Frequency
Print a list of assets and depreciated values	Yearly
Enter newly purchased assets	As needed
Delete assets that have been sold	As needed

Summary

In this chapter, you encountered some basic concepts that should help you understand the overall process of database design. Specifically, you learned that:

- The business-system design process is a cycle that begins with the identification of the end result and continues with the design and implementation of the design. Database design is the foundation for the overall process, and its success helps speed up the movement toward the end result.

- A database design is a document that provides a detailed description in both text and graphics of what the data structures for a business system will look like.

- The database design process starts with the identification of the end result, continues through the development of tables, including the design of fields and table relationships, and ends with an evaluation of the impact of reality on the theoretical design.

- Application requirements include a description of the users, the tasks to be accomplished, and who will be responsible for what task.

- The growth of your business should always be considered during a database design process. Specifically, growth can affect the number of users of a system, the speed with which a system does what it needs to, the volume of data storage required, and how much detail is needed to make the system usable.

- The database design process can be initiated by sitting down and making a sketch, and it can be facilitated through ongoing sketches and brainstorming. The process should always be documented, if through no other means than with simple notes and sketches.

- An important goal of the database design process is the creation of a one-page database design diagram.

3
CHAPTER

Snapshots of the database design process

The database design process encompasses many steps and even more concepts. As a design unfolds—and a good design will tend to make itself known (to unfold) in a very real way—you might find it difficult to keep focused on the end result. There are so many different issues to consider that in some ways database design becomes a challenge landmarked by the difficulty of keeping the different steps in mind and in sequence.

To help prevent the above sort of brain fatigue, this chapter will give you a brief overview of the whole process. The Family database used throughout the book to demonstrate problems, techniques and solutions is used in this chapter to give you a quick set of snapshots of the design process. This procedure will give you the opportunity to focus on the "why" rather than the "what" issues. In addition, this should help focus your attention with a glimpse of what is to come, giving you some perspective on what you're working toward in the end.

These snapshots of the process are provided in a fairly graphic format. Each step is described briefly, the section of the book that addresses the topic is identified, and the implementation of that step is laid out in a diagram. Most of these figures will reappear later in the book at the appropriate time.

Database design step 1: Identify the requirements (see chapter 2, Defining the requirements). Make a list of the inputs and outputs that you expect the database to support. If you have reports or graphs, get copies. Be as specific as possible (see Table 3-1).

Table 3-1 Family-database requirements.

End Result: Manage contacts with family members
Identify a previously met family member, using hair and eye color, height, glasses (or not), and clothing pattern preference.
List all family members' cars by make and model.
List family members without a car.
List families who live in California.
Analyze family members by clothing pattern preferences.
Add a new family.
Add a newly met family member.
Update family member information.
Update member car information.

Database design step 2: Create a master list of info elements (see chapter 4, Creating a master list of info elements). Make a list of all the elements of information suggested by the input and output tasks (see Table 3-2).

Table 3-2 Family database information elements.

Task	Info elements
Identify a previously met family member, using hair and eye color, height, glasses (or not), and clothing pattern preference	Name Hair color Eye color Height Build Glasses Pattern preference
List all family members' cars by make and model	Member name Family Make Model
List family members without a car	Member name Family (no car)
List families who live in California Family Address	Member name

Task	Info elements
Analyze family members by clothing pattern preferences	Member name Family Pattern preference
Add a new family	Family name Address
Add a newly met family member	Family name Member
Update family member information	Family name Member Age Build Glasses
Update member car information	Family name Member Make and model

Database design step 3: Identify the entities (see chapter 4, Dividing the elements into entities). Assess what entity (what object or process) is being described by each info element, group the like elements together, and give each group the name for a table (see Table 3-3).

Table 3-3 Family-database entities.

Info elements	Entity
Name Address Hair color Eye color Height Build Glasses Pattern preference Age	Family member
Family name Address	Family
Car make Car model	Member car

Database design step 4: Identify the primary key (see chapter 4, Assigning a key to the unique element). Figure out which info element makes each thing unique, and define it as the primary key for the table (see Table 3-4).

Table 3-4 Family-database primary keys.

Table	Primary key
Family member	Member ID (surrogate)
Family	Family ID
Family car	Car ID (surrogate)

Database design step 5: Isolate the fields (see chapter 5 sections: Isolating the fields and Naming a field). Take each info element one by one and break it down into nondecomposable components—as individual as they can get. Name each isolated component as a field (see Table 3-5).

Table 3-5 Family-database fields.

Info elements	Field(s)
Name	Member ID
Address	City
	State
Hair color	Hair color
Eye color	Eye color
Height	Estimated height
Build	Build
Glasses	Glasses
Pattern preference	Pattern preference
Age	Age estimate
	Family ID
Family name	Family name
Address	City
	State
	Car ID
Car make	Car make
Car model	Car model

Database design step 6: Describe each field (see chapter 5 sections: Defining a field's datatype, Defining a field's domain, and Reevaluating the fields). Take each field and individually determine the appropriate data type, domain, and rules for the field (see Table 3-6).

Table 3-6 Family-database fields described.

Field	Data type	Domain	Rules
Member ID	Integer	Values 1–500	Unique
First name	C(20)	First names	First letter uppercase, all others lowercase
City	C(20)	US cities	Required
State	C(2)	US states	Required
Hair color	C(8)	Brown, blonde, auburn, grey black, red	
Eye color	C(8)	Brown, blue, black, albino	
Rough height	N	0–100 inches	Rounded to nearest inch
Build	C(5)	Thin, heavy, muscular	Default to thin
Glasses	L	Yes, no	Default no
Pattern preference	C(10)	Patterns	Required
Age estimate	C(10)		Required
Family ID	N	1–50	Required
Family Name	C(15)	Names	Required
City	C(20)	US cities	
State	C(20)	US states	
Car ID	N	1–400	Unique,required
Car make	C(15)	Japanese or Chevrolet	Toyota, Honda, Chevy
Car model	C(25)	(models)	

Database design step 7: Relate the tables (see chapter 6). Identify the type of relationship by analyzing the connection from both sides (see Fig. 3-1), model the connection with the appropriate fields (see Fig. 3-2), and refine the database design diagram to reflect these relationships (see Fig. 3-3).

Database design step 8: Modify the design to reflect the requirements of the environment (if necessary, see chapter 8 through 10). In this example, modification is unnecessary, because the database is so small.

In this example, the snapshots are relatively few, and the resulting design quite simple. Remember that as you move through the book, not all the issues will be quite so straightforward.

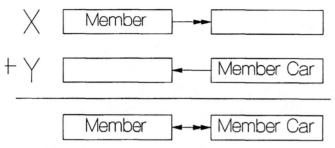

3-1 Looking at both sides of a relationship.

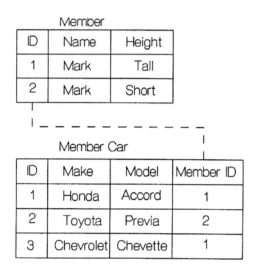

3-2 A modelled one-to-many relationship.

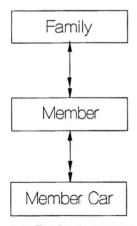

3-3 The Family database design.

Summary

This chapter provided a quick overview of the entire database design process. To summarize, the steps involved in the process include the following:

1. Identify the requirements.
2. Create a master list of information elements.
3. Identify the entities.
4. Identify the primary key.
5. Isolate the fields.
6. Describe each field.
7. Relate the tables.
8. Modify the design to reflect requirements of the environment.

Part 2
Designing a normal database

4
CHAPTER

Developing a table design

Normalization is a term that refers to a specific process that ensures your database tables conform to the rules of the relational model. This section of the book is intended to help you create a normalized database design, but without once using the term normalization. Thus, the database you design through Part 2 will meet the standards of relational theory: each table will be normal, if not specifically normalized. This normal database could be the end result of your database design; although you might want to optimize it (the subject of Part 3), in many cases you won't have to.

By now you probably have a good idea of what is involved in the database design process. You've got the tools in hand for building the design: your pencil and paper are ready to catch the flow of creative ideas. You stand poised to create an application and the documentation that goes along with it.

To provide some perspective, thus far the discussion of database design has focused on the database design environment. You have might feel virtually inundated by all the factors that can affect the design. Now you need to shake off some of that necessary background noise and focus your attention on the heart of any database system: the table designs.

Understanding the elements of a table

You've already encountered the rough-and-ready definition of a table in previous chapters. Now you need to look more closely at this definition. Specifically, what makes up a table?

As discussed in chapter 1, a *table* is a two-dimensional grid of rows and columns. A table contains data about individual occurrences of a specific object or a process. Some DBMSs refer to a table as an *entity*. A table containing data about objects can list data about a person, a place, or a thing. A table describing a process could contain data about purchases, sales, transactions or other activities.

---

table   A set of columns and rows that describes a single object or process and that is the fundamental data structure of any relational database.

A table's name usually describes the object or process in a single word. The table in Fig. 4-1 is named Member; other tables could be called Invoice, Client, Contact, Equipment, or Transaction, to list a few examples.

Column names

Name	Height	Build
Mark	Tall	Muscular
Mark	Short	Thin
Margaret	Tall	Thin
Karen	Tall	Athletic
Diane	Short	Thin

4-1 The Family Member table.

What a row is

A *row* represents a single occurrence of the object or process defined by the table. All of the data in a row are related to that single occurrence. As suggested by Fig. 4-2, each row represents a single member of the family. A row is often called a *record* (in this context, the terms are completely interchangeable). A row is less frequently known as a *tuple*, a term used in relational theory.

Each row in an Invoice table represents an individual invoice; a row in a Client table describes a single client; Contact, one contact with a customer; Visit, one visit by a patient; Equipment, one piece of equipment; and Transaction, one general ledger transaction.

---

row Used interchangeably with *record* to refer to one occurrence of an object or process within a table (the horizontal of the table).

record Used interchangeably with row to refer to one occurrence of an object or process within a table (the horizontal of the table).

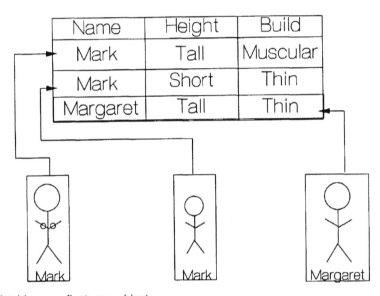

4-2 A table row reflects one object.

Look at this another way. Imagine that you are meeting some members of your extended family for the first time. You want to make note of each new member you meet, so you jot down his or her name. To represent these people in your Member table, you would need to add a new row for each new person that you met. You could create a sketch of this, which might look something like Fig. 4-3.

The table has three rows, one for each person that you've been introduced to. Note that your list shows you've met two people named Mark. In reality, remembering that there really are two Marks is not difficult. All

4-3 Thinking about building the Family Member table.

you need to do is look at them in order to recognize this fact; what's more, in one glance you can easily differentiate between them. Drawing this kind of distinction is impossible for a computer, at least without your providing the mechanism to do so.

What a column is

A *column* represents one descriptive element of each row. In the context of this example, columns are a lot like a list of different adjectives that describe a noun.

Take another look at your list of family members. You want to remember who is who, beyond the fact of each person's name. When you met the first Mark, you assessed what you saw—you described him to yourself. If you had to write this description, you might use adjectives such as tall, muscular, and youthful. Each adjective describes one feature, or attribute, of the person. In the member table that you are constructing, each of these adjectives would be found in its own column, which identifies the feature that is being described. This Member table might have columns like those described by Fig. 4-4.

The column name identifies the feature, while the data in the column

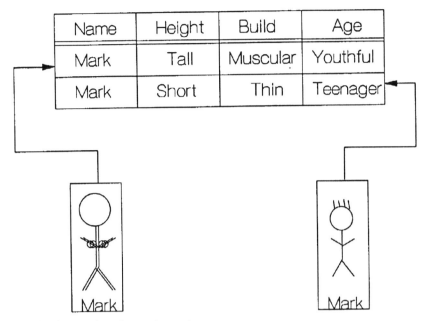

Name	Height	Build	Age
Mark	Tall	Muscular	Youthful
Mark	Short	Thin	Teenager

4-4 Adjectives to describe each member.

describes that feature for a specific individual. All the features in a given row describe one person—in this case, each of the Marks.

You can describe features in terms that go beyond simple adjectives. One of "tall" Mark's distinctive features might be the fact that he wears glasses. Another feature might be the fact that he always wears stripes. Columns are not limited to adjective descriptions; anything that explains or describes the entity (member) can be contained in a column.

Within a single column, the value in every row will be the same kind of data and will describe the same attribute of the row (in this case, the same feature of the family member). Each column should contain data that describes only one attribute. A column is often referred to as a *field*; like *row* and *record*, *column* and *field* also are interchangeably used. Less frequently, a column is called an *attribute*.

---

column   Used interchangeably with *field* to refer to one descriptive element or attribute of a table (the vertical of the table).

field   Used interchangeably with column to refer to one descriptive element or attribute of a table (the vertical of the table).

65

In Fig. 4-5, the Member table has been expanded to include Glasses and Favorite Pattern columns. The columns for an Invoice table may include items such as Invoice #, Customer Name, Address, Equipment Type, G/L Account #, Purchase Date, and Contact Phone Number. The column name usually indicates the type of data that the column contains the "name" of the feature that is being described or identified.

Rows and columns in combination create the grid that is a table structure. Different DBMSs represent this grid to a user in different ways. In some products, a table is bounded by a visible horizontal and vertical grid. In others, the columns of a table are separated by vertical lines, but the rows have no separators. In fact, a grid is not an integral part of a table; it simply helps you to visualize the relationships between the different data elements. Vertical lines, or rules, help reinforce the commonality of each value in a column, while horizontal rules help focus your attention on the fact that all the data in a given record relate to the same entity or occurrence.

RDBMS products define a table much more specifically. In fact, since table is such a well-used term, relational theorists have coined another term entirely to describe a table that conforms to the relational model: a relation.

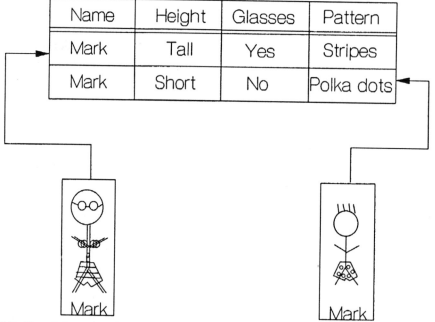

4-5 More information about each member.

What a relation is

A relation is a special kind of table. All relations are tables, but all tables are not relations. More specifically, a *relation* is always a theoretical table that conforms to all of the rules established by the relational model. The relational model currently specifies 14 general rules, and many other specific rules, that a relation must conform to. One of the first general rules specifies "freedom from positional concepts" (Codd 1990, 32). By this rule, a relation identifies each record independently of the next; there is no relative ordering of the rows. There is no such thing as a record being located "next" to another. In other words, each row can be accessed for a specific output without regard to its relative position in the table.

Also by this rule, a relation contains fields that have no relative positioning. The fields are independently named, and they are theoretically unordered. As with a relation's records, a relation's columns have no "nextness."

It would seem that a relation can exist only in theory, because in practice a table that exists will contain rows and columns in a specific order. However, remember that a table doesn't exist in a physical form either—it is only a logical concept. The data being stored physically is always managed by the DBMS in some unimportant way. Thus, it is possible to conceive of DBMS tables that are relations, and in practice to treat these tables under the rules of the relational model.

The goal in defining relational database structures is to develop tables, that is, relations, that conform to the relational model. Consideration of the DBMS that will be used to implement the database design is reserved to the end of the database design process (see chapter 8), and should not have an impact on development of the table designs.

The group of relational tables that jointly form a database design also can be termed a *relational database*. In other words, a relational database is a collection of relations that all work together to define the data involved in a particular business system or a single application (see Fig. 4-6).

One DBMS can be used to create and manage any number of databases, or more to the point, any number of different applications. Because each table in a database remains a separate and unique entity, the question of whether it is a part of a given database is not always easily answered. For this reason, many DBMSs require that each database be given a name, that can be associated then in some way with the appropriate database tables. This association is usually by context only; the data in the table won't refer to it at all. Some DBMSs simply require that all the tables in a single database be stored within one *DOS subdirectory*, a specific area of disk storage. Thus the subdirectory location of a table can provide a clue

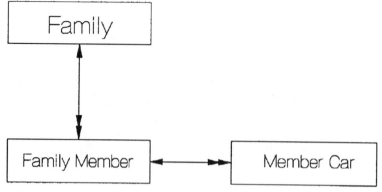

4-6 The big picture of a relational database.

as to the database it is associated with. Part of the power of a relational database lies in the fact that a single table—or even a set of related tables—can be copied or moved from one database to another without any loss of meaning. However, this requires that critical relationships are preserved, and that the database designs are essentially compatible.

Designing the data structures (tables) to support an application is known as the process of *database design* because all of the tables designed will be conceived of as one unit, working together toward the specified goal of the business system: the end result. Thus, the table-design process is more correctly the tables design process; each table in a database should be developed with the scope of the entire database in mind.

An overview of the table-design process

The process of developing table structures takes you in a direction opposite to the processes you've seen before. Although table development begins with the big picture, it immediately leaps into great detail. The big picture is then gradually reconstructed, this time in an organized, relational fashion. Basically, all this overwhelming detail is organized into groups that are formalized, enhanced, and grown to create individual tables (see Fig. 4-7). Overall, you should cover the following steps:

1. Review the business system tasks
2. Create a master list of information elements
3. Divide the elements into entities
4. Determine what makes each entity unique
5. Assign a key to the unique information element

6. Design the fields
7. Identify the table relationships

The first five steps are addressed in this chapter, while the final two often most time-consuming aspects of the process, steps six and seven, are covered in detail in chapters 5 and 6.

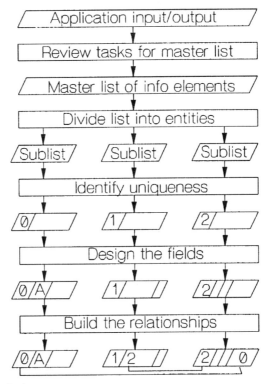

4-7 The table-design process.

Reviewing the application input/output requirements

The place to begin is with your layout of the tasks you intend the application to perform. Each input or output task is in itself a goal. Ask yourself what information you need to achieve this goal. You should find clues to the answer within the statement of the task itself. The more descriptive the phrase that describes that task, the more obvious the answer will be.

Each item of information that you uncover will be called an *information element*, or in abbreviated form, info element. Each info element you identify will have some meaning associated with it. For example, the output task "Print client labels" assumes that you know the right address, but the right address is not just any address; it is the specific address of one (or each) of your clients. The info element is thus not a simple address, but instead a *client address*. Be descriptive; the more detail that you retain at this point in the process, the more likely it is that the application you create will be able to retain it as well. Focus on the information content, not just an item of data stripped of meaning.

 info element (information element)   An item of information that has not yet been defined or broken down into a specific field or fields.

A task that requires printing a report should give you some indication of what that report should look like. What are the info elements you'll need in order for the report to tell you what you want to know? If you are already producing the report manually or with some other system, get a copy of it. If that's impossible, make a sketch. Chapter 8 discusses some tips you can use in the design of new reports.

Give each info element a descriptive name, one that uses your own words and the specific terminology of your business. If your source report already contains some kind of header or name for the element, use it. For example, if you need an employee's name, a simple Employee Name description will be enough detail for now. However, if you need the name for each job the employee has worked on during the period 1/1/88 through 1/1/92, specifying a simple Job # won't be enough. You'll need to make sure you include Dates Worked and Jobs by the Employee as info elements.

Don't overlook information you need to get the task done, but that might not appear on a resulting report or graph. Ask yourself in what order this report will print? Are you assuming that you can sort the information, or will you rely on the computer to do it? A *sort* is simply a rearrangement of values into a specified order, usually following numeric, then alphanumeric order. Is the sort on a value that you've already defined, or on some other value? If you want to see a list of employees in the order in which they were hired, you'll need to know the Hire Date information for each employee. If you want to print your client labels in zip code order, you'll need to have the Zip Code available for each client. Table 4-1 describes the tasks for each case study along with the info elements required to get each task done.

sort   The arrangement of values into a specified order, usually following the ASCII keycode order.

Table 4-1. Case-study tasks and associated info elements.

Task	Info elements
Print a daily/weekly/monthly schedule	Dates covered Date printed Appointment times Appointment clients
Print invoices for clients	Client name & address Invoice date Hours worked Services performed Total due
Display a daily schedule	Current date Appointment times Appointment clients
Display client information	Client name Address Telephone number Primary contact Secondary contact
Enter new appointments	Appointment date Appointment time Client Service to perform
Modify the appointment schedule	Appointment date Appointment time Client Service to perform
Enter client contacts	Client name Client contact Primary or secondary?
Update client information	Client name Address Telephone number
Print a list of purchase orders by user or item category	Purchase order number PO date Vendor User Items Quantities Prices Total PO amount
Print a list of vendors	Vendor name Address Telephone number

Table 4-1. Continued.

Task	Info elements
Print an analysis of processing time by buyer	PO date issued PO date closed Buyer
Enter new purchase requests	User Items Date requested
Modify current purchase requests	User Items Date requested Date updated
Create purchase orders	Purchase order number PO date Vendor User Items Quantities Prices Total PO amount Buyer
Close a purchase order	Purchase order number PO date closed
Display purchase orders by user, vendor, or order date	Purchase order number PO date Vendor User Items Quantities Prices Total PO amount Buyer
Maintain vendor, item, and buyer data	Vendor name Vendor address & phone Item name Item description Buyer name
Print a list of animals	Animal name Age Cage
Print a genealogy for each animal	Animal name Father name Mother name Grandfathers' names Grandmothers' names

Task	Info elements
Print a list of available cage space	Cage Number of spaces available
Enter new births	Date of birth Animal name Mother's name Father's name
Modify animal records	Animal name Cage
Display all available data about an animal	Animal name Cage Mother Father Grandparents
Maintain cage data	Cage name Location Number of spaces
Print a list of assets and depreciated values	Name of asset Depreciated value
Enter newly purchased assets	Name of asset Description of asset Date purchased Purchase price Depreciation period
Delete assets that have been sold	Name of asset Date sold

Creating a master list of info elements

Once you have gone through all the tasks one by one and have identified the info elements for each, you should combine all the info elements into a single list. This list could be quite lengthy, or it could be relatively short. Don't be concerned about the number of info elements, or any relationships between them that might leap out at you. When you first create the master list, you should take care to copy the info elements straight from your list of tasks, and ignore any other concerns. In addition, you should retain your documentation regarding the association of info elements with each task. This documentation will be invaluable when you are ready to actually program, or use the DBMS to define, the tasks.

After you have made the master list, go through the list and mark out those elements that are duplicated elsewhere on the list. Be careful to eliminate only those elements that exactly match. If Client Name appears once and Name appears elsewhere, look closely to see if both descriptions relate to the name for each of your clients. Table 4-2 describes a master list for each of the case studies.

Table 4-2 Master list of info elements.

Dates covered	Primary contact
Date printed	Secondary contact
Appointment times	*Appointment date
Appointment clients	*Appointment time
Client name & address	*Client
Invoice date	Service to perform
Hours worked	*Appointment date
Services performed	*Appointment time
Total due	*Client
Current date	*Service to perform
*Appointment times	*Client name
*Appointment clients	*Client contact
*Client name	*Primary or secondary?
*Address	*Client name
Telephone number	*Address
	*Telephone number

Purchase order number	*User
PO date	*Items
Vendor	*Quantities
User	*Prices
Items	*Total PO amount
Quantities	*Buyer
Prices	*Purchase order number
*Total PO amount	*PO date closed
Vendor name	*Purchase order number
Address	*PO date closed
Telephone number	*Purchase order number
*PO date issued	*PO date
PO date closed	*Vendor
Buyer	*User
*User	*Items
*Items	*Quantities
Date requested	*Prices
*User	*Total PO amount
Items	*Buyer
*Date requested	*Vendor name
Date updated	*Vendor address & phone
*Purchase order number	*Item name
*PO date	Item description
*Vendor	*Buyer name

74

Animal name
Age
Cage
*Animal name
Father name
Mother name
Grandfathers' names
Grandmothers' names
*Cage
Number of spaces available
Date of birth
*Animal name
*Mother's name
*Father's name
*Cage
*Animal name
*Cage

*Mother
*Father
*Grandparents
*Cage name
Location
Number of spaces

Name of asset
Depreciated values
*Name of asset
Description of asset
Date purchased
Purchase price
Depreciation period
*Name of asset
Date sold

At this point in the development of a nonrelational system, you might feel prepared to take each identified info element, turn it into a column or set of columns, and be done. You already have come up with a description of everything you need to know, or more exactly, everything you think the DBMS needs to know. What more is there to do except start implementing?

At this point you should take a step back and review what your goal in this database design process is. You want to create a business system that delivers information of value, information that will help you make a decision. To do this, it is obvious that your application must know what is information of value, and what isn't. You need to be able to rely on your application to tell the difference.

For example suppose you are at the family reunion the year following your first gathering. A man walks up to you—who is he? Because your family member system keeps track of all these people for you, you quickly pose a question to the system: who is this? Your system must be able to sift through all the data floating around and match up all the right pieces. You need to be sure that the name and the descriptive features really pertain to the same person. Obviously, if they don't, you'll be unable to make a good decision and you won't know who this is. If your family member system i still residing in your brain only, you run a risk: you could have forgotte. those connections you built a year ago. However, if you've transferred the information to a computer, the connections will still be intact, and finding the right row (you do know this man is tall and is wearing stripes) will guarantee your coming up with the right name.

Your application will be acting on, that is, finding, manipulating, and retrieving, individual items of data (remember, that is all a computer can deal with), but what you want is information. The only way to make this work is to have you associate the information you need with the data the DBMS will store.

That is exactly the point you are at right now in designing your database. You need to determine how to retain the information content of each info element, while still handing it to the DBMS to manage as data. You know that "2047 Marina Lane" is the address for "MRT Manufacturing," one of your clients (this is information). However, you must apply this knowledge to a table structure that will contain only data.

Remember, in a relational database, everything that is known about the application is contained in tables (and only tables). You must thus define the right column in the right table, a definition that will allow the DBMS—and your application—to always associate that address with that client.

The table structure consisting of rows and columns is all you have to contain the information you want. So you must plan carefully to take full advantage of the intuitive relationships a table provides. Remember that a row contains several pieces of data, all of which describe the same object or process. So if you need to describe an object, use columns in the same table to contain the information. If your application can find the name "MRT Manufacturing" in a table, you can bet that the address the application finds in that same row will be for that same client.

However, there is a hook; an info element that describes one object could be an object in its own right. What if one of the info elements that describes Mark is the type of car he drives, but he owns two cars? How in the confines of a single table can you describe this information? Obviously you've got three choices: 1) two entries into a single column, 2) two separate columns (first car, second car), and 3) a new row containing a different car than the first row. Relational theory calls this kind of information a *repeating group.*

Each method (row, multiple-valued single column, or multiple columns) of expressing a repeating group in a single table causes problems. With multiple values in a single column, the basic table structure of one value per row and column combination is violated. With a new column, the assumption is made that every family member will have the same number of cars, and thus every row for every member will have to reserve space for that (potential) information. With a new row, all the data for that member (name, height, build, etc.), except the name of the car must be repeated in every row, because there is no way in the table itself to associate one record with any other record.

In a relational database, the solution to this problem is straightforward. Each repeating group is broken out into its own table, and a relationship is defined between the new and old tables. In this example, the Member table would be related to a new MemberCar table (see chapter 5 for a thorough discussion of table relationships).

This is by far the most difficult concept in relational database design, and modelling it is the toughest task in the database design process. It can be expressed simply: break the info elements into logical tables. Unfortunately, it isn't simple: how do you know what tables to create, and where to put which info elements?

Dividing the elements into entities

You can break down the process into three distinct steps:

1. Assessing what entity is being described by each info element.
2. Grouping each entity's info elements together.
3. Naming each entity as a single table.

Assessing what entity is being described by each info element

Once you've created a master list of info elements, you should begin to assess which entities are being described by each of the elements. An *entity* is any "thing which has definite, individual existence in reality or in the mind; anything real in itself" (Guralnik, Ed., 1976). An entity can be a Member, or a MemberCar. Each entity that you uncover will be represented in the database design as a separate table.

---

 entity   A thing that has a definite, individual existence in reality or in the mind; anything real in itself.

Remember that in a database design two types of things are usually entities:

1. An object (person, place, or thing)
2. A process (transaction, occurrence, or activity)

Look for similar phrases that are being used to describe different aspects of the same object or process. For example, Employee Name and Employee Address would likely describe two different features of the same entity: an employee. Sales Order Date and Order Amount might well be two different info elements relating to a specific sales order.

If an info element occurs more than once for a given entity, pull it out and create a separate table to hold that information. For example, if a single employee had two dependents, your info elements list would likely contain an element called "Dependents" along with the rest of the information about the employee. You should extract this repeating group and create a new, separate table to hold the information associated with any dependent.

Grouping each entity's info elements together

Once each info element has an identifiable entity associated with it, you should reorganize your master list to bring each entity's elements together. As you continue the database design process, each entity will be identified as a single table, and the info elements you've collected will be the basis for the fields of that table.

Note the continued use of the term *info element* here. Remember, you have not yet broken out the data from the info element. Each info element still contains vital information that you need to preserve in the application. There is no need to bring any arbitrary descriptive data into the system; if there is no need for a data item (there is no information associated with it), then the application should not recognize it or include it.

Naming each entity as a single table

Once you've established the groups of info elements, you need to identify each entity with a unique name. *Naming conventions*, rules for naming that you follow as standard practice rather than by necessity, differ between DBMS products. In particular, different DBMS have different restrictions as to the length of and type of characters allowed in a table name. Many DBMSs store each table in an individual file, and in that case table names must be consistent with the rules imposed on a DOS file name, including the maximum length of eight characters.

---

 naming conventions Rules for naming that you follow as standard practice rather than by necessity.

In any case, a theoretical table name should always be singular: Member and not Members, Employee and not Employees, Client and not Clients, and so on. This is because the table name is intended to describe each one of the rows in the table; one row in the Employee table describes one employee, while a single row in the Client table describes a single client.

Table 4-3 describes the info element groups for each of the case studies. Take particular note of the mistake icon in case study 1 (naming a table with a nondescriptive name). Each table should have a name that is meaningful. The name should provide you and any other user with a sense of what information likely can be found within that table structure. Most of the time the name of a table is fairly obvious. If it isn't, there is a good chance that the information you are trying to lump together really doesn't belong all in a single table, that is, it doesn't describe a single object or process.

Table 4-3 Info element groups.

Table1
Dates covered
Date printed

Table2
Date
Time
Client
Services performed

Table3
Client name
Client address
Telephone number
Primary contact
Secondary contact

Table4
Invoice date
Hours worked
Total due
Services performed

oops!

Naming each table with a nondescriptive name. Rename each table to indicate the entity being described by the table

Table1: Report
Table2: Appointment
Table3: Client
Table 4: Invoice

Purchase order
Purchase order number
PO date
Vendor
User
Total PO amount
PO date closed
Buyer

Items
Item
Quantity
Price
Item description

Vendor
Vendor name
Address
Telephone number

Purchase request
Date requested
Date updated
User

oop∫!

Naming a table in the plural. A table name should always be singular, describing the contents of a single row. Rename the table.

Items: Item

Animal
Animal name
Age
Date of birth
Cage
Father's name
Mother's name
Grandfathers' name
Grandmothers' name

Cage
Cage name
Location
Number of spaces
Number of spaces available

Asset
Name of asset
Depreciated value
Description of asset
Date purchased
Purchase price
Depreciation period
Date sold

Also review the mistake icon for case study 3 (naming a table with a plural name). A table name always should refer to one record in the table, or one occurrence of the entity.

Determining what makes each table unique

Once you've identified the basic tables needed, the next step in the design process is to figure out which info element will be used to describe each row individually in the table. What makes each entity unique? Specifically, what feature of this entity is different for each and every row? What makes each row unique?

Make a note of the selected info element for each table. Each record in the table must be uniquely identifiable with the use of this element. The element you choose to identify each row of a table sometimes is called the *identifier* (or ID) for that table. For example, each employee in an Employee table should be identifiable in some unique way. An employee's social security number might be selected intuitively as a field that could uniquely identify that individual.

identifier (ID)   The field or fields (or during the design process, the info element) that can be used to identify uniquely each row of a table.

The info element that you choose to be the identifier must have (or be assigned) a different value for each record in the table. Thus, an element like a Name would not be appropriate, because a name could be shared potentially by several different people.

A unique identifier is crucial to the design of any table because the identifier becomes the "name tag" for that individual (or specific process or object) throughout the rest of the database design. Because a family member is associated with a specific family, the family's unique identifier is used to describe that association; the member is *tagged* with the family's ID (see Fig. 4-8). Also, if an invoice is created for a specific client, that client is referred to by its unique identifier: the invoice is tagged with the client ID. These cross-references, or *tags*, are the links that define relationships between tables in a relational application (see chapter 6).

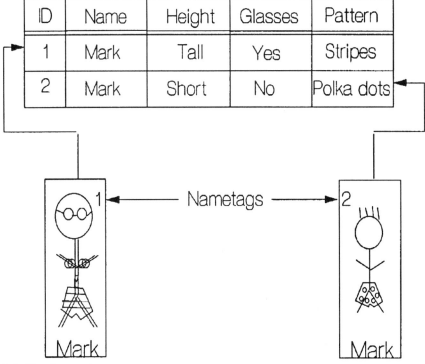

ID	Name	Height	Glasses	Pattern
1	Mark	Tall	Yes	Stripes
2	Mark	Short	No	Polka dots

4-8 Tagging each row.

Assigning a key to the unique element

Because identifying values are used for linking, or tagging, in the examples above, identifiers are crucial to the relational model. In the model, the identifying element for a table (the field in which you find the name tag) is known as that table's *primary key*. (For the purposes of this discussion, a primary key is assumed to be contained within a single field of the table. A discussion of multifield keys is reserved for later, after the concept of atomic field values has been introduced.) Once assigned, a key can be used throughout the database to refer not only to a particular entity but to a specific record in that table; because the key value is always unique, each row in the table is also unique. Remember, an entity is a real thing. In the model, each of these things is tagged with the key value, which is used to refer to that thing everywhere else it is found in the database.

What a primary key does

Most RDBMS support the designation of a primary key for each table. The designation of a primary key usually occurs as part of the table creation or modification process. Once a primary key has been designated for a table, it usually has three impacts on the application:

1. Each record in the table is forced to be unique because the primary key value is forced to be unique.

2. The table will be kept in sorted order by primary key value.

3. Database operations involving the table work faster.

---

 index   A separate and relatively small file used to keep track of values (in the case of a primary index, it tracks primary key values), and which allows a DBMS access to a particular value without searching the table itself.

In general, these three features of primary keys are applicable in most RDBMSs. This is because the standard implementation of a primary key involves the RDBMS creating an *index*, and more specifically, a *primary index,* that is a separate (and relatively small) file used to keep track of the primary key values and where in the table they are located (see Fig. 4-9). Once created, the primary index allows the RDBMS to get at specific records in a table without having to search the whole table itself. (Refer to chapter 7 for a further discussion of DBMS implementation of primary keys.)

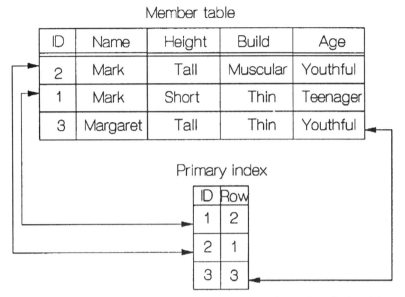

Member table

ID	Name	Height	Build	Age
2	Mark	Tall	Muscular	Youthful
1	Mark	Short	Thin	Teenager
3	Margaret	Tall	Thin	Youthful

Primary index

ID	Row
1	2
2	1
3	3

4-9 A primary index relates the primary key value to its associated place in the table.

Finding the ideal key

There could be more than one info element that uniquely identifies an entity. Each potential primary key value is known as a *candidate key*. Even if there are several candidate keys for a table, only one should be selected. However, how do you choose the best element for the job?

Review for a moment the way a primary key value will be used. Like a name tag, it will appear anywhere (and everywhere) that entity is referred to. In practice, this means that primary key values are often found in more than one table—sometimes even in many tables—within a single database. Because the primary key is used everywhere, a bad key choice can haunt you.

So what is a good key? First, a good primary key is as small as possible (e.g., #1 rather than #100000000). A smaller primary key value will occupy less storage space and will be accessed more easily by the DBMS. The ideal primary key will thus be both short (few characters), and if possible numeric, because in general numeric values (numbers) occupy less space than alphanumeric values (letters or other characters).

Second, a good primary key is unchanging. Remember, the primary key value will be used as a reference to the entity everywhere else in the application. When a primary key value must change, you are forced to make the change not only in one table, but in all the other tables in which the reference to that entity might have occurred (called a *cascading effect*). It is easy to avoid the problem of changing the primary key value by simply making the primary key meaningless. There is usually no incentive to change a value that has no relationship to the real world and that is meaningless. Thus, the ideal primary key should be both meaningless and unchanging.

It might be possible for you to make your life easier by using certain common RDBMS features in conjunction with primary keys. Many applications allow you to depend on the DBMS to keep track of primary keys, even to the point of automatically numbering each new row as you add it. *Autonumbering* is often of great benefit, because it usually provides a primary key close to the ideal: short, numeric, meaningless, and thus unchanging.

 autonumbering   A DBMS function that builds a primary key value without the need for user input.

Using a surrogate key

Some tables might not have an obvious primary key value. In those cases in which an info element does not exist that would make an appropriate primary key, you might choose to create a special element specifically to act as the primary key for the table. This created element is known as a *surrogate key*, because the primary key value is not really an attribute (a feature or description) of the given entity.

Take the Member table as an example. Is there anything in the Member table that you can use to identify uniquely each family member? Is it Favorite Color, or age, or name? Obviously the data doesn't support any of these choices. The solution is to create a surrogate key for the table. You can add a new column to the table to act as this key; Member # would be an obvious column name (or ID, as described in Fig. 4-8). Member # is a surrogate key because it has no existence in reality; it is created and used strictly by the application.

Note that defining a surrogate key should not make your life harder. Many users complain when they have to "keep track of" this kind of meaningless number. It seems to add a layer of complexity to the use of an application. However, a truly relational DBMS will shield the user from ever having to know anything about a surrogate key. If your application requires you to know an employee's number, and cannot accept your information in the way you use it (by employee name, for example), it is more likely a problem with your specific RDBMS than one with your database design. Table 4-4 provides a listing of all the database tables and their primary keys for each case study.

Table 4-4 Tables and their primary keys.

The primary key for each table is indicated by an asterisk (*).

Report
Report ID*
Dates covered
Date printed

Client
Client ID*
Client name
Client address
Telephone number
Primary contact
Secondary contact

Purchase order
Purchase order number
PO date
Vendor
User
Total PO amount
PO date closed
Buyer

Item
Item*
Quantity
Price
Item description

Animal
Animal ID*
Animal name
Age
Date of birth
Cage
Father's name
Mother's name
Grandfathers' names
Grandmothers' names

Asset
Asset ID*
Name of asset
Depreciated value
Description of asset

Appointment
Date*
Time
Client*
Services performed

Invoice
Invoice number
Invoice date
Hours worked
Total due
Services performed

Vendor
Vendor ID*
Vendor name
Address
Telephone number

Purchase request
Request number
Date requested
Date updated
User

Cage
Cage number
Cage name
Location
Number of spaces
Number of spaces available

Date purchased
Purchase price
Depreciation period
Date sold

The next step in the database design process lies in reevaluating the specific info elements in each table. This involves turning the info elements into fields and is the subject of the next chapter (chapter 5). A detailed discussion of table relationships is deferred until chapter 6.

Summary

To review, designing a table begins with an understanding of the table structure itself. You should now be comfortable with the row/record and column/field terminology, and also with the following concepts:

- A relation is a special kind of table that conforms to the rules established by the relational model.
- The table design process begins with an evaluation of the tasks the business system will perform, then continues with a breakdown and regrouping of the information elements suggested by those tasks.
- A master list of info elements must be created that lists out (in no particular order) the items of information that the application will be required to manage.
- The info elements should subsequently be divided into entities that form the foundation of relational tables.
- Each entity identified should then be isolated and named as a single table.
- Each table must then be evaluated to determine what makes it (and each record in it) unique. The unique element is then identified as the primary key for the table.
- A primary key acts as the enforcer of the "uniqueness" requirement of a relational table.
- The ideal primary key is short, numeric, meaningless, and unchanging.
- A surrogate key can be built to help identify each row in a table (to tag each occurrence of an entity).

Overall, a table should describe occurrences of only one object or process; have a descriptive, singular table name; and include only unique records by applying a key.

5
CHAPTER

Designing
the fields

You have several groups of info elements in front of you. Each group, which you have roughly defined as a table, has a name and some element that you have selected (or created) to represent its primary key. These rough groups contain what information you need your application to manage for you.

You probably have guessed that each info element corresponds roughly to a column definition (remember, the terms column and field are completely interchangeable). However, translation of that info element into the precise parameters of one (or more) column definition is more delicate an operation than you might expect. Why is this the case, when a table structure is such an intuitive one, and the name of a column seemingly so obvious?

This question returns you to the truth underlying the entire database design process: it is very difficult to isolate what you know about an item of data from the data itself. A simple description of an info element can come with an entire host of associations that are known to you or other users but are not obvious to your application. The task in defining the field that will contain this data is to build those expectations—those things that you know about the data, or in other words, the information that you know—into the field definition itself.

This process has already begun: you have applied your knowledge of the different info elements to organize them into groups that you believe represent different entities: real life objects or processes. Now you must apply a more rigorous analysis to uncover additional assumptions that you work with and which make the information you know valuable.

An overview of the field-design process

Field design, in contrast to the more common term, field definition, is a term used very appropriately to describe this process. In a very rough sense, you already have completed the field definition; you've identified what you need the system to manage. Remember, however, a field definition only represents a structure for what will be managed. A column that is to hold accurate and useful data must have identified those questions—what is accurate and what is useful?—in the design process. Thus, field design is an art; it involves both skill (how do I communicate my expectations to my application?) and intuition (what do I know that I need to communicate?).

The field-design process begins with the isolation of individual data components from an info element. Figure 5-1 identifies each step of the field design process. Each isolated component, now more appropriately called a field, is then described in detail. The description identifies the name of the field, as well as details about the *field data type* and *domain*. Both of these terms are defined and thoroughly discussed later in this chapter.

Once the field has been described, it must be reevaluated to determine if it is appropriate to the current table. Does this field truly describe the entity? Or does it describe something else—is it dependent on some other value in the table? Refer to Fig. 5-1 as it explores the process of designing fields to contain address information. Once three fields are isolated from the info element Address, each is described by name and type of data expected, and the range of possibilities for the field is exposed. Once each is reevaluated, however, it is clear that two of the fields, City and Zip

5-1 The field-design process.

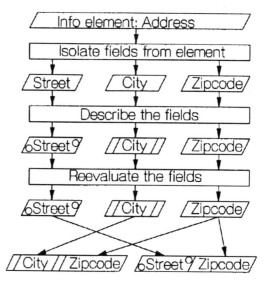

Code, have a relationship that wasn't obvious on first glance. In reality—in real life—the Zip Code field defines the value in the City field. Your zip code and city name are both descriptive of where you live; each zip code area is in effect a subset of each city area. Relational theory thus would indicate that the City field is inappropriately placed in the current table. A solution that conforms better to the relational model would be to create a second, separate table that accurately reflects the dependency. The second table would contain each Zip Code along with the City that is always associated with it (remember, this is still theory, not practice!). The City field would be removed from the current table entirely.

Isolating the fields

Starting with the first group of info elements that you have defined, take a look at each individual info element in turn. Ask yourself if you can isolate any components within this single element while still retaining the meaning associated with it? Relational theory calls this concept *atomicity*, and it is integral to the concept of a relational table.

As defined by C.J. Date, an *atomic value* is one that cannot be decomposed or broken down into any smaller unit without losing the meaning associated with it (1990). I prefer to use the term *isolate* rather than *decompose*, because decomposition implies a loss of value; isolation of different elements, on the other hand, tends to reinforce the concept that each element is independent and valuable on its own (see Fig. 5-2). (Note that the concept of atomicity becomes fairly questionable when applied to more sophisticated types of information such as graphic images or sounds.)

atomicity   A quality of a value that indicates that it cannot be broken down into components without the loss of its meaning.

For example, the Address info element described above does contain three specific components: Street Address, City, and Zip Code. The Street Address component could be broken down into subcomponents (e.g., Street Number and Street Name). If you isolated these subcomponents, however, meaning would be lost, because that meaning is dependent on the order in which the two components appear. The Street Address value only retains meaning, is only accurate and reflective of reality, if the number and street name appear in their proper order, with the proper spacing.

Thus, this first step, which might seem the simplest, is not always straightforward. Refer to Table 5-1 for some examples of field isolation through an analysis of case study 2 (EB).

5-2 Data elements are independent pieces of an info element.

Table 5-1 Isolating the fields for case study 2.

Info element	Field(s)
Purchase order	
Purchase order number	Purchase order number
PO date	Purchase order date
Vendor	Vendor ID
	Vendor name
User	User name
Total PO amount	Total purchase order amount
PO date closed	Purchase order date closed
Buyer	Buyer name
Item	
Item*	Item number
Quantity	Quantity ordered
Price	Price
Item description	Item description
Vendor	
Vendor ID*	Vendor ID
Vendor name	Vendor name
Address	Street address
	City
	State
	Zip code
Telephone number	Area code
	Phone number
Purchase request	
Request number	Request number
Date requested	Date requested
Date updated	Date updated
User	User name

Also note that an atomic value also can be regarded as one that does not exist elsewhere in the database, regardless of the form it might take. In other words, if you can calculate a value based on another value, don't store both. Only the source value is necessary, because you always can construct the other value when you need it. You might note in case study 3 that the Age field is really another version of the Date of Birth field: they represent the same information. The Date of Birth field would be the one to keep, however, because you always can calculate the Age from the Date of Birth; you can't calculate the other way. All the fields for case study 3 are found in Table 5-2.

Table 5-2 Isolating the fields for case study 3

Info element	Field(s)
Animal	
Animal ID*	Animal ID
Animal name	Animal name
Age	
Date of birth	Date of birth
Cage	Cage number
Father's name	Father/animal name
Mother's name	Mother/animal name
Grandfathers' names	Paternal grandfather/animal name
	Maternal grandfather/animal name
Grandmothers' names	Paternal grandmother/animal name
	Maternal grandmother/animal name
Cage	
Cage number	Cage number
Cage name	Cage name
Location	Cage building
	Cage row
	Cage level
Number of spaces	Number of spaces total
Number of spaces available	Number of spaces available

Naming a field

Once an atomic component has been isolated from within an info element, it more accurately can be called a field. The task of describing that field then falls into the two major categories of naming the field and identifying the values that you expect the field to contain.

Creating a descriptive name

First, the field name should be descriptive. Although different RDBMSs do place practical restrictions on the length or type of characters allowable for a field name, a theoretical name should be as complete as possible. Referring back to the Member table described earlier, Age is probably an inappropriate name for the values in that column. Because the descriptive values that are known for the column include Youthful and Teenager, the name of the field more appropriately would be Age Estimate or even Age Attitude. The column describing the Height of each Member more appropriately would be labeled Relative Height or Rough Height, because the values known to be included in the field are Tall and Short (see Fig. 5-3).

If the field name accurately and completely describes what is expected in a column, following the basic relational column-naming rule (RN-3) is easy enough. Specifically, Codd mandates that "all columns . . . within any single relation must be assigned names that are distinct from one another, and distinct from the names of relations and functions" (1990). Thus, if the Member table were to contain another column describing the person's favorite color of shoes, the design would have to take into consideration the fact that Favorite Color already existed as a column, and thus a new column would have to be named more specifically (e.g., Favorite Shoe Color).

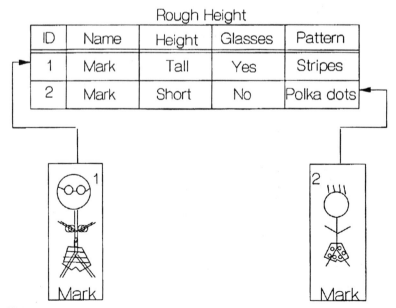

5-3 Field names should be as specific as possible.

Table 5-3 identifies field names for fields in case study 1. Note that the field-isolation process can yield additional fields, or even additional tables, that you didn't even think of the first time around. For example, a given appointment conceivably could cover more than one service, and thus a separate table, Appointment Service would need to be created to handle each specific service that was performed. In another change, the service changed from a descriptive field to a coded field (Service Code) in order to accomodate the numerous times that description would have been required in other tables. Also, Total Due was a value required for the Invoice table, but its source (a billing rate) was nowhere to be found. Thus, Service Rate was added as a new field to contain the rate at which each kind of service would normally be billed (the assumption in this business is that all clients share the same rate for the same service).

Table 5-3 Isolating the fields for case study 1. ☎

Info element	Field(s)
Schedule	
Schedule date*	Schedule date*
Dates covered	Schedule start date
	Schedule end date
Date printed	Schedule date printed
Appointment	
	Appointment number*
Date	Appointment date
Time	Appointment start time
	Appointment end time
Client	Client ID
Appointment service (new)	
	Appointment number*
Services performed	Service code performed*
	Hours worked
Service (new)	
	Service code*
	Service description
	Service rate
Client	
Client ID*	Client ID*
Client name	Client name
Client address	Client street address

Table 5-3 Continued.

Info element	Field(s)
	Client zip code
Telephone number	Client telephone number
Primary contact	Primary contact name
Secondary contact	Secondary contact name
City (new)	
	Zip code*
	City name
	State abbreviation
Invoice	
Invoice number	Invoice number*
Invoide date	Invoice date
Total due	Total amount due
Invoice detail (New)	
	Invoice number*
Services performed	Service code performed*
Hours worked	Hours worked

Because each column name within a given table must be unique, it follows that each combination of table and column name will be unique. As a matter of convention, many DBMSs always identify a particular column (or depending on circumstance, a particular value in a column) relative to its table. Thus, the Favorite Color column from the Member table is described as Member. Favorite Color, with the period indicating (by convention only) the relationship between the table and field names.

Beyond the specified rule, Codd suggests that a column name should contain a reference to the domain from which the column values are drawn (1990) (see the discussion on domains later in this section for details).

Using the singular rather than the plural

Like a table name, a column name is intended to describe one occurrence of the feature being described. More specifically, a column name should describe one atomic value. Thus, the Zip Code field name describes one value in that column: a single zip code. The City field describes one value in that column: a single city name. If more than one value is needed to describe that element for a single row (e.g., a person in the Member table has not only one but two favorite colors), this qualifies the value as a repeating group. As with all repeating groups, a new and separate table should be created to handle that information.

Refer to Table 5-3 for examples of when fields must be broken out into other tables. Note that the breakdown of the Services Performed field requires not only field isolation into individual services performed per appointment, but actually the creation of two new tables: an Appointment Services table and a Services Code table. Also note that the Schedule Date info element required two components, Start Date and End Date, to be isolated. Similarly, the Appointment Time info element required two components, Start Time and End Time, to be isolated.

---

repeating group   The relational model's term for a feature of an entity that can include more than one value.

Defining a field's data type

Once a field has been named, you already should have evaluated the data that you intend to keep in that field, and you are probably familiar with what that data will look like. In effect, both the validity and the appearance of the data will contribute to its value to you as information in your application. To refer back to the earlier discussion, you have knowledge that your field definition must convey to the RDBMS. In this case, that knowledge relates to the values that you expect to find in a given column.

One way to describe each value you expect to find in a column is through a convention known as a *data type*. A *data type* is a description of a value that the DBMS uses as a way to understand some fundamental qualities of that value. A data type is just that: a type, or category, of data. The specific category that you select for each field depends on two factors:

- What a value is
- What the DBMS can understand

---

data type   A description of a value that the DBMS uses as a way to understand some fundamental qualities of that value.

Describing what a value is

There is a difference between what the a value is and how it appears. What a value is falls into a few, relatively limited categories, and in the purest sense reflects nothing more than how we perceive it (bear with me;

this is not an attempt to delve into existential philosophy). We can use any of our five senses to perceive information:

- Sight
- Sound
- Smell
- Taste
- Feel

These categories probably don't look much like any data type that you've encountered in the past. This is simply because the translation of information (in this case, a specific value) into computer-based data is still in a rudimentary phase. Humans are able to perceive information through all five senses, but today's RDBMS products (partially because of the computers they are designed to operate on) are able to understand only a very limited subset of that. Today's computer can know basically only what you can describe in words (and sometimes images), but this cannot reproduce the experience being described.

Once again, the basic problem is that you can make intuitive connections between information received in a variety of forms. A smell can invoke a vivid visual memory, the feeling of a plastic apple easily can change your opinion about whether it would be a good apple to eat, the sound of glass shattering immediately can bring the image of a broken window to mind. Even the most formidable writer would be hard pressed to find language to describe all that you can perceive.

A computer cannot make these intuitive connections. In fact, a computer's language is so simple it has only two words: yes and no. The binary nature of computer processing (literally using only 0 and 1 to describe everything) makes the expression of complex information a matter of thousands of connections—thousands of yes's and no's in combination. Given this context, it is fairly easy to see how this limitation flows over into the types of data that the computer can manage. The more powerful the hardware is, that is, the more thousands, or millions, of connections it can manage at once, the more complex the data is that it can handle.

---

 multimedia   Video and audio capabilities.

Today's RDBMSs support a limited variety of categories of data, basically extending only through the visual (sight) realm. Some computer applications, such as multimedia, are expanding the variety of data types that a computer can handle (currently just into the area of more complex visuals and sound). Most applications, however, still are limited to the simplest of visually perceivable information.

Expressing a value in a way that a RDBMS can understand

In this area of visual information, most RDBMSs support the following specific types of values:

- Numbers
- Text
- Images (sometimes)

To provide you with better support for more specific groups of values within these categories, many RDBMSs create subsets of these, including:

- Floating point numbers
- Integers
- Small integers
- Decimal values
- Dates
- Times
- Dollar values
- Character values
- Logical values (true/false, yes/no, or 0/1)
- Graphics (16-bit characters)

Table 5-4 identifies these different possible data types along with examples of values that might be labeled appropriately with the type. All character data types require that you specify the maximum length of a

Table 5-4 Examples of values for various data types.

Data type	Sample value
Floating-point number	2456.3999 10000.976
Integer	778977 128000097
Small integer	355 20000
Decimal value	255.2 988776.4
Date	1-1-91 6 Feb 1998

Table 5-4 Continued.

Data type	Sample value
Time	10:14:33
	23:18
Dollar value	$8,754.33
	$4.00
Character value	MRT Manufacturing
	To be or not to be:
Logical value	Yes
	0

value that might be found in that field; some RDBMSs require that other data types also be specified with a length as well. The specific types of data that an RDBMS supports has something to do with how it manages the logical-table-to-physical-data translation. Values of different data types occupy different amounts of disk space and make the DBMS do more or less work to manipulate them. In general, numbers are easier to deal with than text values and also occupy less space.

Understanding the difference between data types and formats

Although RDBMSs truly do manage the values of different data types differently, most products also separate how the data is managed from how the data is displayed. The difference can be subtle.

All data types (like Date) actually can control what data is allowable in a field defined with that type. For example, most DBMS maintain an internal calendar against which any date entered into a date field is evaluated—if it isn't a real day, the value is excluded from the field.

A date that is legal, however, can appear in many formats (again, reality versus the computer). A day exists on a calendar (and in real life), but it can be described in several ways—"1/1/91", "January 1, 1991", or "1 Jan 1991", etc. (The use of quotation marks around a value does not follow the assumption made by most RDBMS programming languages that a value surrounded by quotes is a string (text) value. In this usage, the quotation marks simply indicate that within is found a value, regardless of data type.) These different descriptions all represent the same value (the same real thing), but use different conventions to display that value. Each different convention often is called a *format*; like a book's format, it reflects the shape, size, type of binding, paper stock, and type face (cosmetics), and has little, if anything, to do with the contents (see Fig. 5-4). Don't be

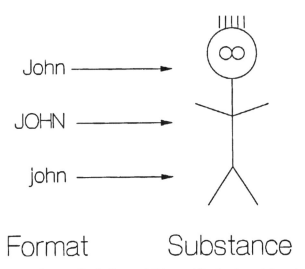

John ⟶

JOHN ⟶

john ⟶

Format   Substance

5-4 The substance of an entity is the real thing, while the format is only a particular appearance of its description.

deceived by the example drawn by Fig. 5-4. Many RDBMSs do differentiate between uppercase and lowercase letters; they are often considered different values. The idea here is just that the different descriptions don't change the fact; what is being described remains the same.

Some RDBMS products draw a fine line between different formats and different data types. For example, a DBMS might manage all numbers the same way; but it also could recognize that you use numbers to mean different things, such as quantities, prices, salaries, ages, etc. Because you are accustomed to seeing currency values with a certain format ($xxx.xx), the RDBMS might assume that all currency values you use should appear in that format, regardless of the underlying nature of the value (which in this case is no different than any other number). Thus an RDBMS might provide you with a currency or dollar data type, which doesn't reflect a true difference in the way the data is managed, but rather supports only a formatting choice.

In any case, the intent of a data type is simply to help you describe the values to appear in a given field. The more specific that description is, the more likely it is that the data that is entered into the field will retain its information content, and that it will be usable as information of value.

Deciding on a data type

Again, the data type for a given field is less a definition than a description of a value. As in most areas of database design, the more specific you can be, the better. Theoretically, all DBMSs, or at least all RDBMSs, should support all potential types of data. Practically speaking, none do.

In creating a theoretical design, however, you should be able to come close. Refer to Table 5-5 for a list of theoretical data types from which you can select. Practically speaking, you probably know which RDBMSs you will be working with. You should utilize the data types supported by that product at this point in the database design process. There is no reason not to apply the specific data types here, if you do know what they are.

Table 5-5 Theoretical data types.

Data type	Abbreviation	Example value
Number	N(2,1)	5.6
number of digits	N(9,3)	888901.983
number of decimal places	N(2,0)	33
Dollar	M(5)	$333.55
number of digits	M(1)	$.07
Character	C(2,F)	Up
number of characters	C(14,V)	My mother . . .
(F)ixed or	C(10,F)	(555)-XRXT
(V)ariable	C(1,F)	z
Graphic	G(1)	[1 picture]
number of characters	G(3)	[3 pictures]
Date	D	3-14-93
month-day-year		2-20-1887
Time	T	11:30:10
hour:minute:second		

Table 5-6 provides a summary of the fields and selected data types for the case studies. Note that zip code values are identified as Character values, even though they can contain only numbers. This is because most RDBMSs specify that numbers cannot contain any leading zeroes; zip codes, of course, have that option.

Table 5-6 Case-study fields and data types.

Field name	Data type
☎	
Schedule	
Schedule date*	D
Schedule start date	D

Schedule end date	D
Schedule date printed	D

Appointment

Appointment number*	N(5,0)
Appointment date	D
Appointment start time	T
Appointment end time	T
Client ID	N(4,0)

Appointment service

Appointment number*	N(5,0)
Service code performed*	N(2,0)
Hours worked	M(2,1)

Service

Service code*	N(2,0)
Service description	C(25)
Service rate	M(5)

Client

Client ID*	N(4,0)
Client name	C(25)
Client street address	C(25)
Client zip code	C(10)
Client telephone number	C(12)
Primary contact name	C(40)
Secondary contact name	C(40)

City

Zip code*	C(10)
City name	C(25)
State abbreviation	C(2)

Invoice

Invoice number	N(5,0)
Invoice date	D
Total amount due	M(7)

Invoice detail

Invoice number	N(5,0)
Service code performed*	N(2,0)
Hours worked	N(5,1)

☞

Purchase order

Purchase order number	N(4,0)
Purchase order date	D
Vendor ID	N(4,0)
Vendor name	C(25)
User name	C(40)
Total purchase order amount	M(9)
Purchase order date closed	D

Table 5-6 Continued.

Field name	Data type
Buyer name	C(40)
Item	
Item number	N(5,0)
Quantity ordered	N(9,0)
Price	M(6)
Item description	C(15)
Vendor	
Vendor ID	N(4,0)
Vendor name	C(25)
Street address	C(25)
City	C(25)
State	C(2)
Zip code	C(10)
Area code	C(3)
Phone number	C(8)
Purchase request	
Request number	N(4,0)
Date requested	D
Date updated	D
User name	C(40)
Animal	
Animal ID*	N(4,0)
Animal name	C(20)
Date of birth	D
Cage number	N(4,0)
Father/animal name	C(20)
Mother/animal name	C(20)
Maternal grandfather/animal name	C(20)
Paternal grandfather/animal name	C(20)
Maternal grandmother/animal name	C(20)
Paternal grandmother/animal name	C(20)

Cage

Field name	Data type
Cage number*	N(4,0)
Cage name	C(20)
Cage building	N(3,0)
Cage row	N(2,0)
Cage level	N(1,0)
Number of spaces total	N(2,0)
Number of spaces available	N(2,0)

Asset

Field name	Data type
Name of asset	C(30)

Depreciated value	M(8)
Description of asset	C(100)
Date purchased	D
Purchase price	M(8)
Depreciation period	N(4,0)
Date sold	D

Defining a field's domain

Beyond the description of the values in a column that you have identified as a data type, the theoretical model supports an additional description of the values. This extended description is actually much more precise than a data type, which is normally just a rough description of what is expected.

What a domain is

A *domain* is a concept so precise that it assumes each and every possible value for a field can be known—and specified—at the time a field is created. In fact, a domain is nothing more than a pool of values from which actual values in the field can be drawn (Date 1990) (see Fig. 5-5). This assumes that there is a distinct difference between a domain (in effect, a separate set or table) and a field (one use of the domain).

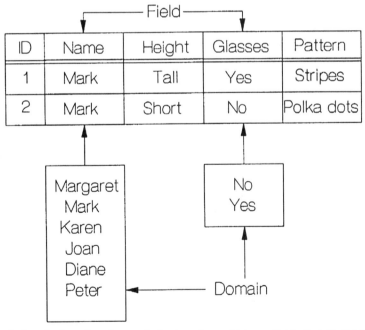

5-5 Each domain describes the pool of values from which any field value must be drawn.

domain   The pool of values from which actual values in a field might be drawn.

Working from the general towards the specific

Domains have been labeled *extended data types* because they extend the description that a data type provides into a greater level of detail. Conceptually, a domain provides the most powerful tool in an RDBMS for retaining information content within a data element. The theoretical importance of this cannot be overstated. When domains are enforced, the RDBMS maintains control over what values are allowable or not. When control is maintained at that level, comparisons between values in different fields become possible. If you know that the Family Name in the Member table comes from the same domain as the Family Name in the Family table, you can make a meaningful comparison between the values. Support for domains give the data manipulation features of a RDBMS a firm theoretical foundation.

Reusing a predefined domain

Although domains are not supported by most RDBMSs on the market today, you should still consider applying the concept to your database design. After you've described a field with a specific name and data type, expand on the description by analyzing what specific values (not just categories of values) you expect to find in the field.

An important support for domains that might not be obvious is through the relational nature of your database design itself. Assume, for example, that you have broken your Member and MemberCar information into two separate tables, as suggested. The MemberCar table will have to include the Member's ID (the name tag for the family member who owns the car). In order for the name tag to be valid, it must exist already in the Member table. In other words, the Member table defines the domain for the allowable Members. This kind of relationship is explored more fully in chapter 6. For now, suffice it to say that relationships depend on domains.

Specifying additional restrictions

Outside of the concept of support for a "list" of allowable values (domains), many RDBMSs support more specific descriptions of field values than those provided by the data types. In particular, analyze your field for the following qualities:

- Range of values
- Unique values
- Required values
- Expected formats
- Defaults

These additional features of a field often can be described in an entirely separate process from the creation or modification of a table. However, they should be conceptualized at this point in the design. Note this kind of feature can be inherent in the value itself or can be enforced as a matter of business policy. For example, in the example of the MemberCar, one field you want to track is the cost of each car owned by the Member. Thus you design a Car Cost field. You might recognize the fact that no value in the Car Cost field will ever be lower than $5000, but the reason for that truth is debatable. On the one hand, it could just be a matter of fact (i.e., no car on the market today costs less than $5000). Or it could just as easily be a business rule that is being enforced (i.e., no one in this family is allowed to buy a car that costs less than $5000). Regardless of source or intent, the range of values is still valid.

Range of values

Do the values in the field always fall into a specified range? Specified ranges usually are based on one of the five mathematical comparison operators—equals, greater than, less than, greater than or equal to, or less than or equal to. These operations are indicated by the standard mathematical signs: $=$, $>$, $<$, $>=$, or $<=$. These operators are used to compare the value in the field with the range limit specified. If a range is specified to be >5, an attempt to place a 4 in the field always should be prevented by the RBDMS.

A range can be applied against any one of many different data types, including dates, numbers, currency values, or even alphanumeric (character) strings. Most RDBMSs support a specific order for characters, usually based on the ASCII key-code order, a standard sort order for the United States that sorts numbers before uppercase characters, which are before lowercase characters. Sometimes you can specify a range such as $<F$ that would imply a range of uppercase characters which came before the letter F. Similarly, ranges can be applied against dates, with the understanding that if date 1 is "less than" date 2, date 1 occurs first on the calendar.

Uniqueness

Refer back to the discussion in chapter 4 on primary keys. One feature of a relational database is that a given table can contain more than one candidate key, but only a single primary key is allowable. A value is only a candidate key if it is naturally found to be unique for each row in a table. If this is a quality of a particular field, you should identify it at this point. Many RDBMSs can support a requirement for uniqueness on a field. Again, the point is to shift as much of the burden as possible to the RDBMS for retaining the information content of a data value; if the value is incorrect, clearly it has little or no worth to an application, and thus to your need for information of value.

Required and missing values

One of the most difficult dilemmas in relational theory focuses on the issue of how to handle values that don't currently exist. In relational terminology (and practically speaking, as well), a field that is left empty in a particular record is said to contain missing information. This can occur in either of two circumstances:

- The value is not currently known.
- The feature does not apply to the current row.

These are two distinctly different situations, but most RDBMSs deal with them using the same technique: allowing a null in place of a value. A null is a special kind of marker, theoretically different from a blank (which is a value) or a zero (also a value). A *null* is used to represent the fact that information is missing. The current version of relational theory discusses this problem extensively but provides few workable solutions, and none that can be implemented given today's RDBMS.

The problem stems from the nature of a table itself. The logical structure of rows and columns assumes that the same set of columns exist for every row in the table. This means that the RDBMS must keep track of every column in every row, regardless of whether that column has a value, or whether that value is an applicable one. This has an impact in three areas:

- Resource requirements
- Accuracy of any query
- Calculations

Resource requirements   The need to keep track of "empty" columns has an impact on the use of both disk storage space and processing resources, including memory. As a result of the tendency of relational theory to break tables into their smallest components (the least number of fields), most RDBMSs work optimally on tables that have few columns. Each additional column adds a layer of complexity to the processing, and thus involves more resources, which has impact on both speed and cost (see chapters 9 and 10).

Accuracy of any query One important reason for applying domain and other restrictions to a field is to help ensure that each value in a field is both valid and true. A null immediately raises both questions. Is it valid?. In other words, is it legal for the value to not exist, or are you waiting to discover the value, and is it true (does the feature just not apply)? Without a method for distinguishing between the two situations, a question asked about a particular table could yield an inaccurate result.

For example, if you wanted to know how many family members had blue cars, you might query the Car Color field of the MemberCar table to extract all those records that indicated a Car Color equal to "Blue." Presumably, the RDBMS would locate all the records with "Blue" in that field and ignore the records without "Blue," including those with nulls. Assume the result indicated that there are five family members with blue cars. You could not be sure that five was an accurate answer to your question, because a null value in that column could represent an unknown color for a member's car that in reality was blue (the correct answer to your question thus would have been six, not five). Based on the model, the RDBMS should have specified the answer in the context of the information that was currently known, such as "Five blue cars, one car of unknown color." This kind of result is, however, impossible in current RDBMS products if the question does not explicitly ask for "unknowns" to be included.

Calculations

In addition to the variance you must accept in extracting data when null values are allowed, you must be prepared to encounter similar variances when attempting to perform calculations on the data. If the question you were asking was what was the total cost of all the blue cars, rather than how many blue cars, any null could have a serious impact on the result.

Beyond simple summaries, there is the well-known problem with multiplication and division operations that affect zero values. This problem is extended when these operations are attempted on a value that doesn't exist, or a null. Many RDBMSs allow the application to control how a null (or a blank) is treated in the context of a calculation (as a zero or not).

You can eliminate the problems encountered when nulls are allowed by forcing the users to enter a value in each field of a table. Most RDBMSs allow a field definition to include a rule that forces the entry of a value (precluding nulls). This might solve the problem of missing-but-applicable information (you just can't enter a record until you uncover any missing piece). However, this doesn't address the problem of missing-and-inapplicable information. You potentially could use a special character to indicate that value (n/a for "not applicable" has been used in this type of situation to good effect, but of course this doesn't work in a non-alphanumeric field).

Defaults

The alternative to forcing a value to be entered in a field is to rely on the RDBMS to enter the value for you. Here, *default* is simply a value that is entered automatically into a field if you have taken no action to add a value on your own. Most RDBMSs support the definition of a field value default as part of the field design process.

Formats

Many values achieve meaning through their internal organization, or the way they are formatted. The example of the Street Address field explored this briefly in an earlier discussion. A street address has meaning because it associates the street number with the street name in a particular order and with a particular spacing. In this sense, the format of the value contributes to its meaning. Thus, the field design should incorporate that meaning into the field by defining (and enforcing, if possible) the expectation for that format.

The power to enforce the format of values, and specifically to enforce formatted text values, varies widely from RDBMS to RDBMS. Some support format specification to the level of each character. Others support formatting only to the level of specifying when breaks in a text field are allowable (much like identifying the required spacing).

In any case, it follows that the more specific a format requirement can be, the more likely it is that the value (information) will retain meaning even when found in that field (data).

Table 5-7 summarizes the various kinds of restrictions, while Table 5-8 describes the domain and appropriate restrictions that should be applied to the fields in the case studies.

Table 5-7 Types of field restrictions.

Specified range
Unique values only
Required value (no nulls allowed)
Default value
Format requirements

Table 5-8 Case-study fields, domains, and restrictions.

Field name	Data type	Domain	Restrictions
Schedule			
Schedule date*	D	No sundays	
Schedule start date	D		< End date
Schedule end date	D		> Start date
Schedule date printed	D	No sundays	<= Sched. date
Appointment			
Appointment number*	N(5,0)		
Appointment date	D	No mondays	
Appointment start time	T		> 8 AM
Appointment end time	T		< 9 PM
Client ID	N(4,0)	Client table	
Appointment service			
Appointment number*	N(5,0)	Appt. table	
Service code performed*	N(2,0)	Service table	
Hours worked	M(2,1)		
Service			
Service code*	N(2,0)		
Service description	C(25)		
Service rate	M(5)		>$45,<$145
Client			
Client ID*	N(4,0)		
Client name	C(25)		
Client street address	C(25)		
Client zip code	C(10)	City	
Client telephone number	C(12)		
Primary contact name	C(40)		All caps
Secondary contact name	C(40)		All caps
City			
Zip code*	C(10)		
City name	C(25)	US only	
State abbreviation	C(2)	US only	
Invoice			
Invoice number*	N(5,0)		
Invoice date	D		1st or 15th of month
Total amount due	M(7)		Sum of hrs*rates
Invoice detail			
Invoice number*	N(5,0)	Invoice	
Service code performed*	N(2,0)	Service	
Hours worked	N(5,1)		from appt. times

Table 5-8 Continued.

Field name	Data type	Domain	Restrictions
☞			
Purchase order			
Purchase order number	N(4,0)		
Purchase order date	D		
Vendor ID	N(4,0)	Vendor	
Vendor name	C(25)	Vendor	
User name	C(40)		All caps
Total purchase order amt.	M(9)		Sum of PO items
PO date closed	D		>PO Date+60
Buyer name	C(40)		All caps
Item			
Item number	N(5,0)		
Quantity ordered	N(9,0)		>=100
Price	M(6)		>1.00,<500
Item description	C(15)		All caps
Vendor			
Vendor ID	N(4,0)		
Vendor name	C(25)		Upper & lower case
Street address	C(25)		
City	C(25)	US city	
State	C(2)	US state	
Zip code	C(10)		Zip plus four
Area code	C(3)	Valid AC	
Phone number	C(8)		Three plus four digits
Purchase request			
Request number	N(4,0)		
Date requested	D		
Date updated	D		>Date requested
User name	C(40)		User from PO
🐃			
Animal			
Animal ID*	N(4,0)		Sequential
Animal name	C(20)		
Date of birth	D		
Cage number	N(4,0)	Cage	
Father/animal name	C(20)	Animal	
Mother/Animal name	C(20)	Animal	
Maternal grandfather/ animal name	C(20)	Animal	
Paternal grandfather/ animal name	C(20)	Animal	
Maternal grandmother/ animal name	C(20)	Animal	

Field name	Data type	Domain	Restrictions
Paternal grandmother/ animal name	C(20)	Animal	
Cage			
Cage number*	N(4,0)		
Cage name	C(20)		
Cage building	N(3,0)		<43
Cage row	N(2,0)		<10
Cage level	N(1,0)		<4
Number of spaces total	N(2,0)		
Number of spaces available	N(2,0)		
Asset			
Name of asset	C(30)		Upper & lower
Depreciated value	M(8)		Price-price*DP
Description of asset	C(100)		
Date purchased	D		>1/1/88
Purchase price	M(8)		
Depreciation period	N(4,0)		12-mo. increment
Date sold	D		>date purchased

Reevaluating the field

Once a field has been defined and thoroughly described, it is important to take a second look at the field and how it relates to the table at hand. One of the problems with the rough technique for isolating info elements into tables explored in chapter 4 is that these info elements aren't very specific until they are designed into fields. It is only after the fact that you can take the opportunity to tell—in the most specific context—whether a field truly describes a feature or attribute of the given table. Or more specifically, the question to be asked is: does the value in this field depend on the primary key value for this row in my table? If the relationship between the field value and the primary key value is not one of dependency, the field probably is incorrectly placed in the table. By definition in relational theory, all columns in a relational table must contain values that each contribute to the description of the primary key (practically, of the entity described by the table name).

As suggested by Fig. 5-1, the rearrangement required to detach an incorrectly placed field from its intuitive table assignment can involve the building of an entirely new table.

Brief review of multifield keys

Now that you've taken a look at the difference between an element of information (info element) and a field definition, it should be clear that the selection of a primary key value in the previous chapter was some-what premature. A primary key must be applied to the field (or set of fields) that uniquely identify a row. The info element identified previously as a primary key might subsequently have been isolated into more than one field. If this has occurred, you need to revisit the issue of the primary key for that table.

Specifically, you need to analyze each field that resulted from the info element identified as the primary key. A primary key that is applied to multiple fields, also termed *multifield, concatenated,* or *composite key,* requires that all the fields act equally in defining the unique quality of that row. By definition, if any field can be removed from the key and not have an impact on the uniqueness of the key, then that field should not be included as part of the key. In other words, a primary key should be defined on the column or *minimum set* of columns that ensure uniqueness for each row in a table.

---

 multifield key   A primary key that is applied to multiple fields.

Including nonkey fields in only one table

This overall process of isolating atomic components into fields and fields into tables might seem like overkill. However, remember that the relational model has its basis in relational algebra, which follows precise rules in order to achieve results that are unambiguous. Given the defined properties of numbers, you can confidently predict that adding three numbers together—in whatever order you choose—always will yield the same result (e.g., 1+2+3=6, 3+1+2=6, or 2+3+1=6). The goal in database processing is the same: you want to be confident that no matter in what form or order you phrase a question, the results you receive will always be the same. So you create fields that have defined properties (i.e., data type, domain, uniqueness, etc.) to ensure that when you work with the values in the fields, you will always get the correct results.

Even if each of your fields are described accurately and thoroughly a particular uncertainty is added when information that you know to be the same is found in more than one place in your database. Excluding the use of primary key values, the name tags that are used deliberately to represent actual things throughout the application, all other information is represented most precisely when there is only one place (one table-and-field combination) for it to exist. For example, if one family lived at a single address, and if all the individual members of that family lived at that address as well, it would benefit the database to include the address information only in one table (Family) but not the other (Member). These benefits accrue for three reasons:

- Ambiguity is reduced.
- Maintenance tasks are simplified.
- Disk storage is conserved.

Reducing ambiguity When information can be located in one and only one place, the question of which is most accurate or up-to-date will not exist. If you need that information, you go to the sole source. There is no need for a debate of any kind.

Simplifying maintenance When a field contains the only description of a feature in the entire database, then if that feature changes, you are able to predict precisely which description you will need to change. Your database will remain more accurate, and will contain more information of value, if maintenance of each field value can be controlled rigorously.

Conserving disk storage Finally, locating a value in only one field will reduce the application's use of disk storage. It is intuitively obvious that storing a value five times will utilize five times the disk storage space than just storing it once. Although intuition isn't completely accurate in this case, the underlying concept does hold true. In general, resources are conserved if each value is found in one field only.

Summary

In this chapter you have reviewed the process of field design, which focuses on the translation of the information that you know about a value into a field structure that the application will be able to manage. Specifically, you have learned that:

- The field-design process covers the development of an accurate description of what is expected in a field: the field name, data type, domain, and other restrictions on any value in the field.
- Field design begins by isolating the fields from within previously defined info elements.
- A field should be named descriptively in the singular.
- A field's data type should represent the most specific option from the range of possibilities.
- A value exists independently from how you describe it; formatting

is simply cosmetic and doesn't change the nature of the feature being described.

- Today, RDBMS products provide limited support for descriptions outside of the written for columns that contain data more complex than numbers, dates, or text.

- A field's domain is nothing more than a pool of values from which any actual value in the field will be drawn.

- A field definition can describe the allowable values in specifics outside those of a domain, including the range of values, the uniqueness of a value, whether a value is required or how it is to be handled if missing, defaults, and formatting options.

- Once a field is designed, it should be reevaluated to make sure that the defined assumptions still hold true.

- Nonprimary key fields should be stored only in one table in order to reduce ambiguity, simplify maintenance, and conserve disk storage.

6
CHAPTER

Relating the tables

Your tables are looking like tables now: each has a name, a primary key, and columns that describe in detail each feature of the entity in which you are interested. Thus far you have taken care to be as specific as possible, closely evaluating the information you work with to ferret out the nuances and subtleties that provide information of value and differentiate this information from valueless data.

Early on you looked at the big picture. Although you still might be working with the sketch of your application you then drew in front of you, you're probably lost in the detail by now. There is no doubt that focusing on the specifics is a sure way to lose sight of your goal.

This last step in designing a table pulls you from that detail perspective, back out to the big picture. Take a look at the several different tables you have designed (see Fig. 6-1). By definition, each exists independently of any other, but that isn't the way you work with them. You deal with, that is, think about, maintain, question, react to, the information in those tables as if the whole was one (or maybe several) integrated unit(s). In this context, *integrated* refers to the existence of a mechanism, or path, by which a database can deal with different groups of information at the same time. A database design must allow and plan for this kind of integration.

The database-design process carefully has isolated the data, one value from the next, and one table from the next. In a sense, thus far you have accomplished one half of the necessary translation: you have translated what you work with into data, values that the computer can manage in a structure it understands. However, now you must create the means for translation from the other side; you need to define the means by which the computer will translate what it knows into what you want. You need to create the mechanism for integration, the paths between tables (see Fig. 6-2).

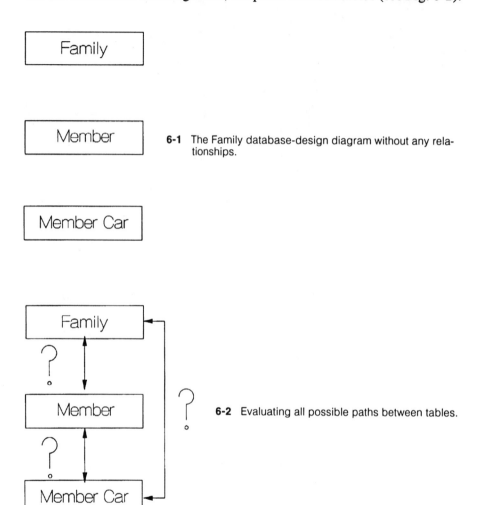

6-1 The Family database-design diagram without any relationships.

6-2 Evaluating all possible paths between tables.

What a table relationship is

By definition, relational databases capture all the information in an application solely within a table or tables. Thus, it is not a difficult task to deduce that this additional type of information, the paths necessary for integrating the tables, will be found in the tables themselves.

In relational terminology, a path for integrating tables is called a *rela-*

tionship. Each relationship is defined between two and only two tables and reflects the existence of a real-life connection between two entities. A relationship is created—and only works—when there is a real connection.

 table relationship   A path created by data that is used to integrate two tables together.

For example, take the two tables, Member and MemberCar. The MemberCar is intended to represent the existence of a car (or cars) that belong to a given Member of the family. There is a true relationship between a given car and a person, that is, the person owns the car. Thus, there should be a relationship defined between the two tables to reflect this fact (see Fig. 6-3). In order for the values in the tables to be useful to you, there must be a relationship defined.

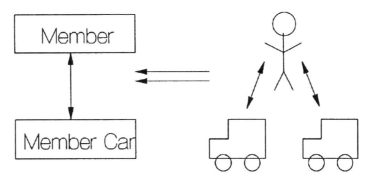

6-3 A relationship between tables always should reflect a relationship in real life.

Identifying types of relationships

There are different ways of defining a path between two tables, and the technique chosen depends on what kind of relationship is being drawn. There are three relational models for real-life connections to describe the three types of relationships that can exist between tables:

- One-to-one
- One-to-many
- Many-to-many

Each type of relationship has two components: x and y, or more exactly, x to y (see Fig. 6-4). Each component reflects one side of the relationship, or

117

one perspective on what kind of relationship it is. The x side is the perspective from one table, the y side from the other table. X and y are interchangeable in the sense that a one-to-many and a many-to-one relationship are (in theory) exactly the same. This idea is examined more fully later in this chapter.

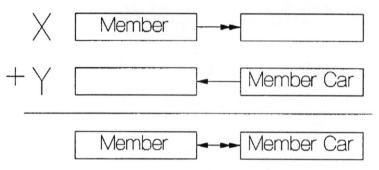

6-4 A relationship must be evaluated from both sides individually.

Although the descriptions of these different types of relationships can seem arbitrary, the selection of a type is not. The type of relationship must describe the actual kind of connection that exists between the real- life entities.

One-to-one

A *one-to-one relationship* exists between two entities when there is (and can only be) a single connection. For example, in your family database you created a table called Member to describe each member of your extended family. If you wanted to provide additional information about the husband or wife of each member, you could create a table named Spouse to describe that person who is related to the member. Each Member at most can have one Spouse; each Spouse can be related (in marriage) to only one Member. Thus, the relationship between the two entities is termed one-to-one. Because one row in the Member table represents a single member (or in the Spouse table, a single spouse), there is a direct connection between a single row in one table and a single row in the other (see Fig. 6-5).

One-to-many

A *one-to-many relationship* exists between two entities when there exists the possibility for connections between one entity in one table and several entities in the other. For example, in your family database your MemberCar table describes the car or cars owned by each Member. There is a relationship between the two (described in more detail immediately above). This relationship is termed one-to-many because one Member can own one or more (many) cars, but one MemberCar can be owned by only one Member (see Fig. 6-6).

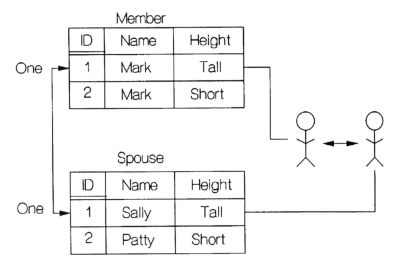

6-5 A one-to-one relationship.

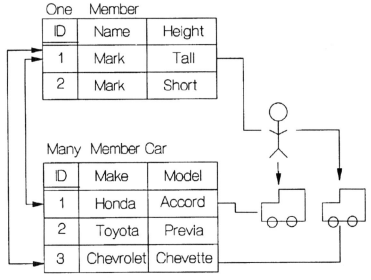

6-6 A one-to-many relationship.

Many-to-many

A *many-to-many relationship* exists between two entities when there exists the possibility for multiple connections from both table's perspectives. For example, a given family might allow multiple family members to share ownership of one car. Thus, one family member could own more than one car (one-to-many from the Member side), but one car could be owned by more than one family member (one-to-many from the MemberCar side). This dual relationship is termed many-to-many and is the most complex kind of relationship to model (see Fig. 6-7). In other words, most RDBMS products have difficulty in managing this kind of relationship.

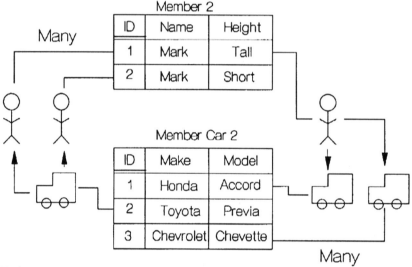

6-7 A many-to-many relationship.

Modelling the connection

Each of these types of relationship describes a connection between two real things, not two tables. In effect, the relationship that will be defined by the database design is not a relationship at all, but is only the potential for a relationship. In other words, the database design must allow for a potential connection between two entities, without requiring that the connection exist.

This concept uncovers one of the most powerful features of relational databases. The potential for the connection exists in a table structure, while the connection itself exists in the actual records in the table. Thus the data—not the structure—defines the relationship (see Fig. 6-8).

This makes the power in the relational model threefold:

- Relationships between entities can be dynamic, reflecting reality.
- Relationships that don't exist don't invalidate those that do.
- The potential for a relationship can be created or removed with simple column functions.

---

 data-based relationships A quality of a relational database that sets it apart from other types of databases. The data is used to make connections.

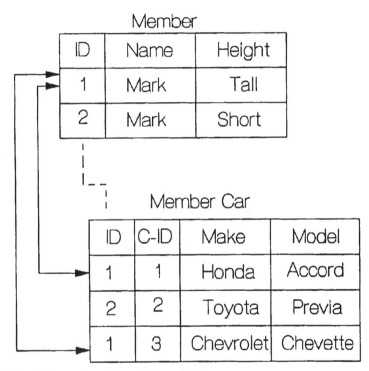

6-8 Relationships are based on matches of data.

Dynamic relationships

What this means is that the information associated with the data can be dynamic; it can change to reflect the real world. If a Member owns one car, there is a single car in the MemberCar table and a single connection between the tables. If the Member buys another car, a second record is added to the MemberCar table, and now there are two connections

121

between the tables. If a Member sells all her cars, all records are deleted from the MemberCar table, and now *there is no relationship at all.*

None-to-none (relationships)

Thus, the potential for a relationship also allows for the possibility that there is no relationship. One-to-one more accurately should be called none-or-one to none-or-one, and one-to-many could be called none-or-one to none, one, or many. The relational design allows you to express information (this Member doesn't own a car) with the absence of data (see Fig. 6-9).

Member

ID	Name	Height
1	Mark	Tall
2	Mark	Short

Member Car

ID	C-ID	Make	Model
1	1	Honda	Accord
3	2	Toyota	Previa
1	3	Chevrolet	Chevette

6-9 A link without a relationship.

Column-based links

The data that actually forges the connection between tables must be located in the tables (where else?). The connection is actually made when the same data exists in both tables. The mechanism the relational model employs to make the connection is the match of data.

How does the RDBMS know, however, where to look for a match? A relational database design plans for this—in effect models the relationships—by including the same column in both related tables. Thus, the relationship between the Member and MemberCar tables is modeled by including the common element—what in reality is the same—in both tables. Because the Member and MemberCar tables both relate to the Member table, the Member's ID field is placed in both tables to allow for a match (look back at Fig. 6-8). This process is pursued in greater detail below.

Two tables that include a common column intended to allow for a relationship between entities are said to be *linked tables*. The potential for a relationship is called a *link*.

 link   The potential that exists for a relationship between two tables by virtue of their sharing a common column.

A link is always built the same way: one of the common columns is a primary key, and that same primary key relocated into the linked table is the common column on the other side. In other words, you use the name tag for one entity to tag the related entity. A primary key, when it is located in a linked table, is known as a *foreign key* (see Fig. 6-10). Foreign keys are thus the basis for all links in a relational database design.

 foreign key   A primary key value when used in another table.

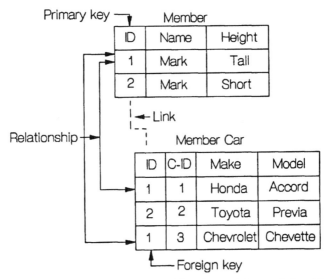

6-10   Common columns create a link; matching data creates a relationship.

The process of building a link

A link between tables is created in several steps:

1. Identify the connection and sketch the boxes.
2. Analyze from one side.

3. Analyze from the other side.
4. Refine the sketch.
5. Define the common column.

Identifying the connection

The connections that you need to identify should be as close as your documentation about the tasks you need to accomplish. Review the initial list of tasks that you created at the beginning of the database design process. Take a look at the info elements associated with each task; what tables are these elements now a part of?

Remember, what you are attempting to do is create the opposite side of the translation process. You isolated the elements for the application, and now you need to reconnect the pieces. The connections aren't arbitrary; they are built on the needs that you already expressed quite clearly up front.

Once you've looked at the list, identify the relationships needed for each task, one pair of tables at a time. You'll note that several of the tasks will be utilizing similar relationship pairings. Table 6-1 identifies each task for the case studies and describes any tables that task requires.

Table 6-1 Case-study tasks and table(s) required.

Task	Table(s)
Print a daily/weekly/monthly schedule	Schedule
	Appointment
Print invoices for clients	Client
	City
	Appointment
	Appointment service
	Invoice
	Invoice detail
Display a daily schedule	Appointment
Display client information	Client
	City
Enter new appointments	Appointment
	Appointment service
	Client
Modify the appointment schedule	Appointment
	Appointment service
	Client
Enter client contacts	Client
Update client information	Client
	City

Task	Table(s)
☞	
Print a list of purchase orders by user or item category	Purchase order Item
Print a list of vendors	Vendor
Print an analysis of processing time by buyer	Purchase order
Enter new purchase requests	Purchase request Item
Modify current purchase requests	Purchase request Item
Create purchase orders	Purchase order Item
Close a purchase order	Purchase order
Display purchase orders by user, vendor, or order date	Purchase order Vendor Item
Maintain vendor, item, and buyer	Vendor Item
Print a list of animals	Animal Cage
Print a genealogy for each animal	Animal
Print a list of available cage space	Cage
Enter new births	Animal
Modify animal records	Animal Cage
Display all available data about an animal	Animal Cage
Maintain cage data	Cage
Print a list of assets and depreciated values	Asset
Enter newly purchased assets	Asset
Delete assets that have been sold	Asset

Take special note of one requirement for case study 3 (Zoo) not directly identified in Table 6-2 but implied through this process, in particular, the identification of the relationships between a specified animal and its parents and grandparents. This is a special kind of repeating group within the Animal table, one that has a consistent number of entries: every animal must have two parents and four grandparents. In effect, you have two choices. Either you can relate the table to itself, which would use the Animal ID for each relative in the principal animal's record, or you could create a separate table for ancestors that would pull out all those columns (mother, father, paternal grandmother, etc.) into a separate table. This might not be the obvious place in the design process to have identified this problem, but it is more common than not to have unusual issues and creative ideas pop up in the oddest places. Take a look at Table 6-2 for a revised take on the tables for case study 3.

Table 6-2 Revised tables and fields for case study 3.

Table	Field
Animal	Animal ID* Animal name Date of birth Cage number
Ancestor	Animal ID* Ancestor animal ID* Type of ancestor
Ancestor type	Type of ancestor Description of ancestor
Cage	Cage number Cage name Cage building Cage row Cage level Number of spaces total Number of spaces available

Look at the tables that are indicated as being required for a single task. It is likely that these tables share a natural relationship—one that the real world dictates—because if they didn't, they probably wouldn't be covered within a single task. If more than two tables are required, look at each potential pair to determine whether there is a direct relationship or not. Then draw a pair of boxes connected by a solid line for each pair of tables. Even if you haven't determined that a relationship exists, going through the following steps will help.

Enter the name of one of the two tables in each box. Figure 6-11 describes a sketch for one pair from case study 1. Remember that you will be going through this process once for each pair (yes, that could be a lot of times through—it just means you'll get really good at analyzing relationships!).

Analyzing the connection from one side

Pick one table of the pair. Imagine that you are in that table. From that perspective, how many entities in the other table could relate to you?

6-11 A pair of tables for case study 1.

Think of a specific example, and jot down on the side under your table box the instance you are imagining. Make a note under the other table box for each potential connection you can imagine. Is there only one possibility? Then draw a 1 in a circle above the other table. Are there many possibilities? Then draw an M in a circle above the other table (see Fig. 6-12).

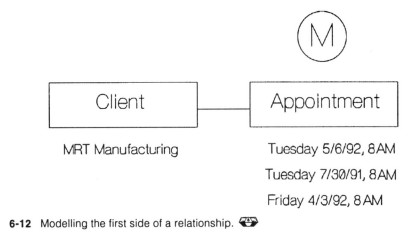

6-12 Modelling the first side of a relationship.

Analyzing the connection from the other side

Choose the other table of the pair. Imagine that now you are in that table. From this new perspective, how many entities in the first table could relate to you in this table? Repeat the steps above, identifying the opposite side of the relationship with a 1 or an M in a circle over the first table (see Fig. 6-13).

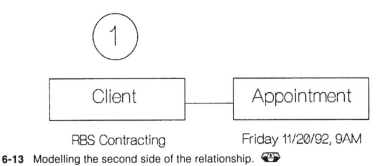

6-13 Modelling the second side of the relationship.

Refining the sketch

A standard technique for describing table links is by connecting the linked tables in a database design diagram with a solid line (as you did above). Each line drawn represents one link. The line then can be enhanced to describe the type of relationship being represented: the 1 side of a relationship will have a single arrowhead pointing toward that table, while any M side of a relationship will have two arrowheads pointing toward that table. In your sketch, replace the circled 1 and M with the appropriate arrowhead(s) (see Fig. 6-14).

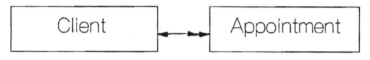

6-14 A relationship diagrammed.

Identifying the common column

Now that you've identified the link, all you need to do is make sure that the columns are in place to contain any matching data. You might discover that in many cases, the necessary columns already exist in the appropriate tables. The fact that you've formalized their usage in this way won't affect your data; it will just make you aware of all the potential relationships that you might want to exploit at some later date. Even if you don't need to use a relationship immediately, having it predefined gives you the flexibility to change your mind. Remember, relationships aren't arbitrary; they reflect true connections in the real world. So your including a link you might not need right away does nothing more than more fully describe your information (which was one of the goals identified up front).

Deciding which column should be the common value between tables is not always straightforward and depends on the type of relationship that has been identified.

One-to-one links

Figuring out which column should be in common is not a problem when the relationship being modelled is one-to-one. The primary key for either table effectively can be used as the common column. Select one of the primary key columns and add it to the other table. Theoretically, either choice will produce in the same result.

In practice, it is often better to evaluate the two tables to determine which is more important in the overall scheme of the database. Most database systems depend on a relatively limited number of important tables that describe the mission-critical aspects of the business. A relational design ordinarily will have many other tables that are created as a result of relational theorizing, information important in concept but of less inherent information value. If a one-to-one link involves an important table and a not-so-important table, placing the common column into the less important table is likely a better choice, because it keeps the number of columns in the important table to a minimum (see Fig. 6-15).

Member

ID	Name	Height
1	Mark	Tall
2	Mark	Short

Spouse

ID	Name	Height	Mem.ID
1	Sally	Tall	1
2	Patty	Short	3

6-15 A modelled one-to-one relationship.

One-to-many links

One-to-many links should be modelled by placing the primary key from the one side of the relationship into the table that is on the many side. In effect, this ties each potential many (in the MemberCar example, each car) to the associated one (the Member who owns it—see Fig. 6-16).

Member

ID	Name	Height
1	Mark	Tall
2	Mark	Short

Member Car

ID	Make	Model	Member ID
1	Honda	Accord	1
2	Toyota	Previa	2
3	Chevrolet	Chevette	1

6-16 A modelled one-to-many relationship.

Many-to-many links

Many-to-many links are modelled by building what is commonly referred to as a *cross* or an *intersection table*. This table is composed of the primary keys from both tables on both sides of the relationship. For the family with multiple owners of cars, the tables might be reidentified as described in Fig. 6-17. Member 2 remains its own table, while MemberCar 2 now really reflects only car-specific information and thus is renamed Car 2. A new intersection table, Member by Car, is created that describes what relationships are valid between the Member and Car tables, that is, which Members own which cars, as well as which cars are owned by which Members. Figure 6-18 demonstrates how an intersection table actually is used to support these relationships.

Summary

In this chapter you have reviewed the process of modelling table relationships. You have evaluated the differences between an actual relationship (existing in real life) and a modelled relationship (a link) that only provides the potential for a relationship to exist. In addition, you have found that:

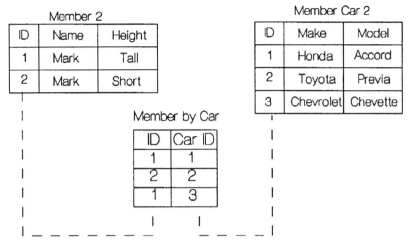

6-17 A modelled many-to-many relationship.

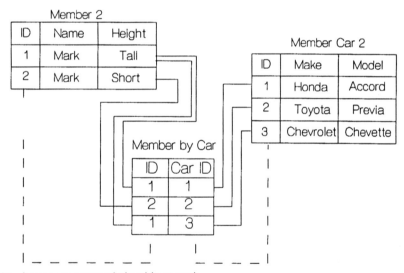

6-18 A many-to-many relationship at work.

- There are three types of relationships: one-to-one, one-to-many, and many-to-many.

- A relationship is created through matching data found in both tables, making each relationship dynamic and allowing for a relationship not to exist at all without affecting the application.

- A link is built through a column common to both tables, and is constructed of a primary key and its duplicate in the linked table as a foreign key.

- The process of building a link follows several steps. First, the connection is identified and sketched, then the connection is analyzed from both sides, and finally the common column then is identified and placed in the appropriate linked table.

- The common column chosen differs depending on the type of relationship being modelled.

7
CHAPTER

Establishing data integrity

You now have in front of you a database that covers the entire spectrum of your information. You have defined the tables, described each column in great detail, and created the necessary links between tables. You should be prepared for the next phase of database design where you consider the impact of reality on this theoretical product.

Before you move on to practical considerations and away from a focus on relational theory, it is important to take one more look at this process of translating the information you work with into data that the computer will manipulate. The process of database design so far has focused on the issue of describing your expectations for the data. You've identified where you think relationships exist, what ranges and qualities are associated with any given value, and which values describe which entities. You should have some good documentation in hand regarding all of these issues.

However, your expectations about the data and the data itself might vary widely. In that case, what happens when they do? From the point of view of the database design, how should you be handling these expectations, beyond just writing them into your documentation?

This chapter addresses the issue of ensuring that your design expectations are met. In it you will revisit the different areas where you should have defined rules for your data, and you will reformulate those possibly loose rules into a set of constraints that most RDBMSs immediately can implement.

Identifying integrity requirements

What is at issue here is *data integrity*. This term is discussed with great seriousness in data processing circles, and is one of those magic words that separates you (the user) from them (the professional-computer experts). The concept is really quite simple: the integrity of your data is a subjective measurement of its value. Value in this sense refers to how useful the data is to your application (and to you).

Integrity usually is measured on a scale (see Fig. 7-1). One side of the scale reads "Low" or "Poor;" this means that your data is so inaccurate, invalid, and out-of-date that it is useless in helping you make any decision. In effect, it doesn't reflect reality. The other side of the scale reads "High" or "Excellent" and means that your data is so useful that you not only depend on it to answer any questions you might have, but you rely on it to help you make decisions; you are confident that it reflects the truth of your business environment. As Fig. 7-1 suggests, the integrity of the data in an application reflects a balance between "good" and "bad" data—that which is correct and that which isn't. Your goal as the database designer is to do whatever you can to tilt the scales in the "good" direction.

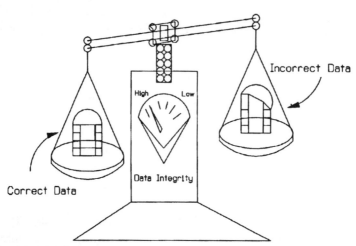

7-1 The data-integrity scale.

Another way of describing this continuum is to take a look at those over-used terms, data and information again. Data whose integrity is "excellent" retains a large portion of its information content—its meaning—even as the application is managing it. Data whose integrity is "poor" has lost its information content and has thus become useless.

You as the database designer must take all the appropriate steps to ensure the integrity of the data; if you don't, the users certainly will not. This is not (particularly) the result of industrial sabotage. Data integrity becomes degraded, or compromised, as it is usually described, from natural forces much more frequently than by any deliberate act. Data entry errors, forgetfulness in following through with all data changes related to a single real-world occurrence, uncontrolled or unvalidated movement of data between different systems; all can have a disastrous effect on data integrity.

Understanding integrity types

There are three basic types of integrity that must be preserved. These three different areas of database design are all impacted by the need to maintain meaning, specifically where the value of an application's data can be lost.

- Entity integrity
- Referential integrity
- Field integrity

Ensuring entity integrity

Entity integrity refers to how accurately a table reflects actual entities in the real world. For a table to meet relational standards (which are intended to preserve integrity), each row must reflect a different occurrence of the object or process in the real world. One real thing must equal one record in that entity's's table (see Fig. 7-2).

---

 entity integrity How accurately a table reflects actual entities in the real world.

This requirement is enforced in the design through the designation of a primary key. If you haven't identified a primary key for each table, you've fallen down on your job as a designer. You are in effect opening the door for questions: is this really the John Doe I want, or is it another John Doe's phone number that I am calling? Does my summary report accurately average all the purchase prices of cars that are blue, or does it count some of them twice, giving them more weight in the average?

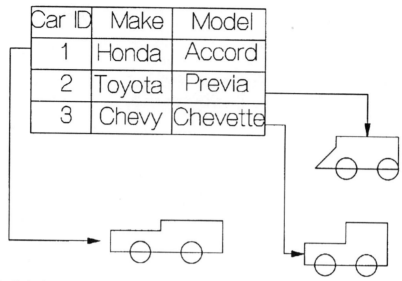

Car ID	Make	Model
1	Honda	Accord
2	Toyota	Previa
3	Chevy	Chevette

7-2 Entity integrity: one real thing per table row.

Ensuring referential integrity

The second issue of integrity addresses how accurately the database reflects real-world relationships that exist between different entities. *Referential integrity* is sometimes called *relational integrity*, because it is what allows you to perform relational activities, such as a join, on your tables and have confidence in the results. Relational activities are basically those that allow you to recombine or access data from multiple tables to achieve a single goal or perform a single task.

---

 referential integrity (sometimes **relational integrity**) How accurately the database reflects real-world relationships that exist between different entities.

Because all relationships in a relational database are created through data in the tables, data errors can destroy relationships crucial to the functioning of the application. Data that doesn't match within common columns, but which should match because there is a real connection, will cause unexpected and incorrect results in many operations. Theoretically, referential integrity is ensured through the maintenance of the primary key-foreign key relationship of any link. By definition, a foreign key value cannot exist (and thus there can be no link) if the foreign key value doesn't already exist as a primary key value in the linked table (see Fig. 7-3). Practically speaking, most RDBMSs don't provide much support for this kind of integrity, and thus a tight coupling of linked relational tables during usage in an application is necessary.

Name	Address	Family #
Smith	Jackson, MS	1
Jones	Kent, WA	2
Reynolds	Wash, DC	3

Name	Height	Build	Family #
Mark	Tall	Muscular	2
Mark	Short	Thin	1
Margaret	Tall	Thin	2
Karen	Tall	Athletic	3

7-3 Referential integrity: one relationship per real-life connection.

Ensuring field integrity

Field integrity is a measure of the value of a description relative to the actual fact that it is describing. Each field is intended to contain an atomic value that reflects a "truth" in the real world—a quality or attribute of the entity that it describes (a quality or attribute of that particular record in the given table—see Fig. 7-4).

Field integrity is impossible to ensure, even in theory. At some point you have to rely on the value to determine whether it is true or false; the application (or the RDBMS) can't do that for you. However, the RBDMS can ensure that the field value is something like what you know it should be.

---

 field integrity A measure of the value of a description relative to the actual fact it is describing.

Depending on domains The fact that each field should be declared (and based) on a specified domain helps. This is the roughest kind of insurance, because a domain basically is unqualified; all potential values in the domain's pool of values are created equal, and whether one is more likely better than another for a given row is not known to the domain (see Fig. 7-5).

137

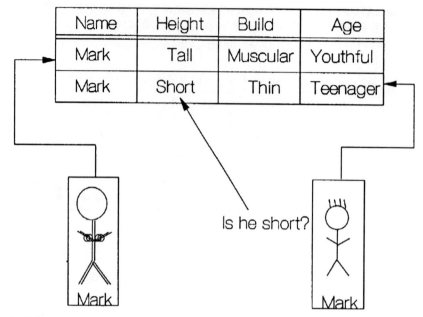

Name	Height	Build	Age
Mark	Tall	Muscular	Youthful
Mark	Short	Thin	Teenager

Is he short?

7-4 Field integrity: is the value in this field true?

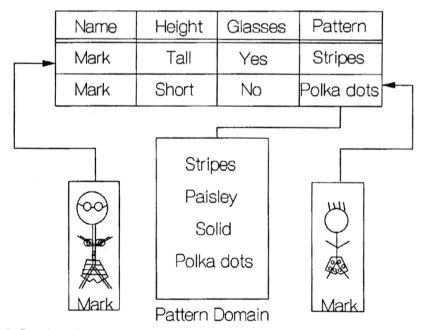

Name	Height	Glasses	Pattern
Mark	Tall	Yes	Stripes
Mark	Short	No	Polka dots

Stripes

Paisley

Solid

Polka dots

Pattern Domain

7-5 Domains in field integrity.

Defining other business rules The definition of business rules is particularly important to the integrity of the data, because these rules tend to be more specific than the features of the data described by a data type or even through a domain.

Most commonly, a business rule describes a real fact that the business depends on in order to function properly. For example, a rule might exist that prevents the price for a particular service from increasing faster than 10% per year. Or a rule might exist that requires new employees to take two community college courses during their first two years on the job. A business might require a potential client to do at least $300,000 in gross annual sales before they will take them on. Or a business could require all employees to undergo a physical exam between the ages of 48 and 51. These kinds of rules don't fit neatly into the concept of a domain, nor do they have an impact on the type of data that a field is intended to store. Instead, they apply the same restrictions to the database as are applied to the real entities in the real world.

Describing this kind of rule in a database design is relatively simple; all you need to do is include it on the design document specifying the field definitions. However, enforcing it through the RDBMS can be quite difficult. Why is this such a challenge for a RDBMS? You know it must be a challenge because the level of support for this kind of feature is so low among RDBMS products.

When data integrity is important

Part of the reason that maintaining data integrity is not a simple task is because all the rules—data type, domain, restrictions, business rules—must be enforced at the point that they could be compromised. In other words, the integrity of the data must be protected at those times in an application when data can be added or changed. Because part of the power of a relational database lies in its flexibility—and particularly in its support for views, each of which potentially uses a different selection of fields from the relational tables—an application that intends to enforce data integrity must do so in a wide variety of situations.

The problems with data integrity are addressed directly by a system that is *object oriented*. Roughly speaking, object orientation refers to a method of dealing with data that defines both the data and its behavior at the same time. In this situation, object orientation would embed the business rules (and data type and domain and restrictions) in the definition of the object (roughly the table) itself. Therefore the object—not the application—would be the enforcer of the rules, which you can immediately see would simplify the application quite a bit.

In particular, an application must examine the data for violations of the rules in three contexts:

- Adding data
- Making changes to current data
- Deleting data

Adding data

Any data which is being entered for the first time obviously must be checked to make sure it meets all the requirements. In an application that depends on data entry from a user at the keyboard, the checking can be done right on the spot (when the value is entered, it is checked). In most RDBMSs, checking like this is implemented fairly easily.

However, many databases depend on data that is entered through a "back-door"—not from a user but from another database or software. Databases that integrate PCs and mainframes often are linked directly through an import-export procedure. Data that is added to the relational tables in this way is sometimes more difficult to examine, because ordinarily you must examine it in a batch mode, corresponding to the way the entries were made in the first place. This kind of checking can be quite complex.

Making changes to current data

Any time that you allow a user (or the application itself) to make changes to the data, you also must allow for the possibility that the changes can violate a rule or rules you have established. Thus, any activity in the application that involves data modification also must allow for a checking process to occur. Again, if the changes are being made by a user one record at a time, the checking is not likely to be very difficult to implement; but if the changes are being made in batch mode through updates from another database, implementation could be much more difficult.

Deleting data

You might wonder how the deletion of data can affect the integrity of the database; it seems as if the validity of the value is really a moot point once it has been deleted. However, recall that integrity falls into three categories: entity, field, and referential. *Referential integrity* describes the validity of relationships, which are based on data found in two tables. Therefore, making changes to data in one table—including deleting data from that table—can (and should) directly affect the data in another table.

This means that previously valid data can become invalid entirely as a result of the modification of another value. It is a particular problem when a record is deleted from the "one" side of a one-to-many relationship. Suddenly, any "many" records that were connected to the deleted "one" record are left stranded. These unconnected "many" records are called *orphans* in relational terminology. Orphans can cause ongoing problems for an up-and-running application, partly because they can be very difficult to find and eliminate once that relationship has been broken.

 Orphan record A record once on the "many" side of a one-to-many relationship whose "one" related record has been deleted.

Relational integrity should thus be of great interest at every point in an application that supports any change to the data in a table, such as through the addition of new data, the editing of current data, or the deletion of data. How this is enforced depends on the RDBMS you are working with, but the description of what needs enforcing should be provided by the database design.

Documenting integrity requirements

The requirements for each field in a table should be identified and described in the design document that specifies field criteria. This document is more than supporting detail for the one-page design document that describes each table and its relationship(s) to the other tables. The field specification is a necessary extension to the one-page document; without it, a design cannot be implemented.

Review Table 5-8 for the complete field specifications for the case studies.

Summary

This chapter reviewed the concept of data integrity that was introduced in several previous chapters. This review should have reinforced several important aspects of maintaining data integrity, including the following:

- Integrity requirements must be identified during the design process and addressed for each table and field in the design.

- Integrity falls into three categories: 1) entity (each record in a table is unique); 2) referential (each record which should be related to a record in another table is related); and 3) field integrity (each value in a field accurately represents the true description of the entity).

- Domains are an important tool in maintaining field integrity; if properly used, a domain substantially increases the probability that a value in a field will be correct.

- Other restrictions to the data should be defined to reflect specific requirements of the business. These rules tend to be unrelated to a pool of values (like a domain) or simple restrictions (like a range). Instead, business rules can combine data from several fields or even several tables in order to ensure the validity of a single value.

- Data integrity is important at any point in an application in which data can be changed, i.e., where data has been added, modified, or deleted.

- Integrity requirements should be documented as part of the database design.

Part 3
Optimizing a database design

8
CHAPTER

When reality strikes: The database environment

Okay, so you're finally done with the theoretical stuff. You have thought and drawn and considered and evaluated and reevaluated until you've conceived a design that will guarantee the integrity of your data. You are prepared to base the most mission-critical decisions of your business on the data in this database.

Well, wake up and smell the roses. No RDBMS exists today that can take your wonderfully relational and perfectly specific design and implement it without modification—not on a mainframe, not on a minicomputer, and most definitely not on a PC.

Even if there was a RDBMS that was fully relational that conformed to all the rules of the relational model, you probably still wouldn't implement your design just as it currently stands. There are too many factors outside the database itself—in the database environment—that you must consider.

Choosing practice over theory

The relational model is intended to provide the parameters for constructing an ideal database in an ideal environment. The theory assumes that everything it is important for you as a database designer to know is covered in the rules—and everything else is handled by the RDBMS. In fact, the current version of the relational model provides rules for "everything else," too (i.e., guidelines for the developers of relational-database-management systems). These rules are thorough, although only to the extent that their effects are visible to the user (or to the person managing the database, known as the *database administrator* or *DBS*). The idea is that as a database user/designer, you will be relying on the RDBMS to manipulate the environment; if your design choices are consistent with the model and your DBMS is relational, the result will be an ideal system.

---

 database administrator (or **DBA**) The person who manages the database and applications.

The theory places great reliance on the capabilities of the RDBMS. Not only does it assume the RDBMS will provide the functionality required to be consistent with the model, but the theory also assumes that the RDBMS will be usable, that is, that it will handle the actual input and output of an application adequately. However, the huge assumptions in "adequately" hit home in two areas:

- Performance
- Cost

Both of these issues depend on considerations not directly related to the theory at all, and both can have as dramatic an impact on the end result as the theory itself. These two issues are addressed in detail in chapters 9 and 10.

Assessing the relational state of your DBMS

An attempt to make a nonrelational DBMS do what a relational design requires would be a disaster. Yet it is well-documented that there still exists a gulf between theory and practice, between the relational model and any DBMS products on the market (Date, 1990). You are a user of a product that is advertised as relational—and a designer of an application based on the relational model. It is crucial that you be able to evaluate where your chosen product differs from the model, and thus where you will need to modify your design to accommodate the difference(s). In order to make this kind of assessment, first you need to take a closer look at the definition of a relational DBMS.

To restate the simple definition given in chapter 1, a relational database is one that is perceived by its users as tables (and nothing but tables). A relational database (tables only) need meet nothing more than this definition. However, a relational-database-management system (RDBMS) must go beyond the simple definition and modification of relational tables; it must also be able to manage—to do meaningful things with—these tables. As suggested by Fig. 8-1, the relational model actually addresses the guidelines for a relational DBMS in three areas:

- Data structures
- Operations on data
- Data integrity

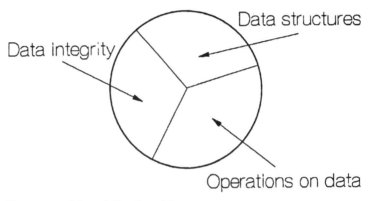

8-1 Three parts of the relational model.

In fact, although the model defines an RDBMS very precisely (what do you think all those 300 plus rules are there for, anyway?), almost all of the rules fall neatly into one of these three categories. Because of the well-documented gulf between the theory and the state of the market, in 1982 Codd suggested a revised definition for relationality, which granted that a system could be relational even if it didn't match the theory in every detail (Codd, 1982). A DBMS thus can be considered relational to the degree that it meets the standards in the three basic areas.

Evaluating a minimally relational DBMS

A DBMS that is relational to the smallest degree is said to be *minimally relational*. Codd suggests that this type of system must provide support for the following two features:

- Relational tables (data structures)
- The most basic relational operations (restrict, project, and join)

147

Relational tables, of course, follow the standard that there is nothing known in the database that is not known as data in the tables. Relational operators, on the other hand, follow the restrictions of relational algebra. These three operators are graphically described in Figs. 8-2 through 8-4. Very roughly speaking, a *restrict* allows a user to extract rows from a table based on some specified condition (see Fig. 8-2). A *project* allows a user to extract specified columns from a table (see Fig. 8-3), and a join allows a user to combine rows and columns from two tables based on data common to both (see Fig. 8-4).

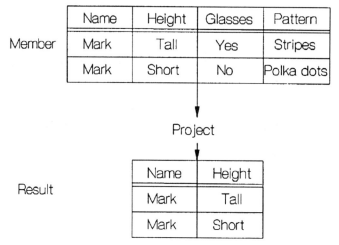

	Name	Height	Glasses	Pattern
Member	Mark	Tall	Yes	Stripes
	Mark	Short	No	Polka dots

Restrict

	Name	Height	Glasses	Pattern
Result	Mark	Tall	Yes	Stripes

8-2 Basic relational operations: restrict (select rows).

	Name	Height	Glasses	Pattern
Member	Mark	Tall	Yes	Stripes
	Mark	Short	No	Polka dots

Project

	Name	Height
Result	Mark	Tall
	Mark	Short

8-3 Basic relational operations: project (select columns).

Family

Name	Address	Family #
Smith	Jackson, MS	1
Jones	Kent, WA	2
Reynolds	Wash, DC	3

Family Member

Name	Height	Build	Fam #
Mark	Tall	Muscular	2
Mark	Short	Thin	1
Margaret	Tall	Thin	2
Karen	Tall	Athletic	3

Result of Join

Name	Height	Build	Fam #	Name	Address
Mark	Tall	Muscular	2	Jones	Kent,WA
Mark	Short	Thin	1	Smith	Jackson
Margaret	Tall	Thin	2	Jones	Kent,WA
Karen	Tall	Athletic	3	Reynolds	Wash,DC

8-4 Basic relational operations: join (combine tables).

---

restrict A relational operation that extracts specific records from a relational table.

project A relational operation by which specified columns are extracted from a table.

join A relational operation that combines tables and brings rows together based on common values.

There are three other "defined" degrees of relationality that Codd also specified in 1982: a *tabular* system (e.g., specifically nonrelational) is one that supports relational data structures (tables) but doesn't support any relational operations. A *relationally complete* system is one that supports relational data structures and all the relational algebra operations (beyond the basic three), and a *fully relational* system is one that supports all three areas—data structures, operations, and data integrity—in their entirety (see Fig. 8-5). It is easy to see that relationality is really a spectrum into which any DBMS may fall, and on which you must judge your (R)DBMS.

The bottom line is that the more relational a DBMS is, the easier your relational design will be to implement. The less relational the DBMS, the more difficult the implementation. In a nonrelational system, the implementation of a relational design will be impossible or certainly close to it. This is because a relational design depends on the RDBMS to be able to do table manipulations in order to bring the fields and records (data values) back into the appropriate real-life combinations.

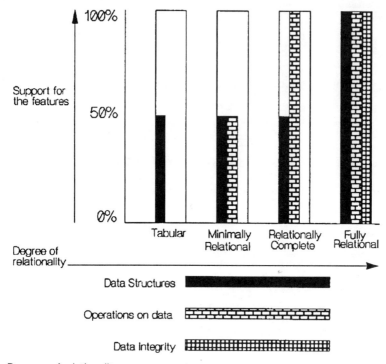

8-5 Degrees of relationality.

The next sections of this chapter will lay out the basics of the relational model in each of the three areas. These summaries provide no justification for the rules (refer to the Bibliography for numerous writings on that subject); instead, the focus here is on allowing you productively to assess how your DBMS measures up to the model.

Measuring DBMS support for a feature

First, understand that this is not necessarily an objective process. Simply asking whether a feature is supported by your DBMS (and expecting a yes or no answer) is misleading. There are definite complexities involved in any implementation. You would do better to ask several questions:

- Does the DBMS allow me to do this (but I'll get hurt)?
- Does the DBMS allow me to do this (and I'll benefit)?
- Does the DBMS help me to do this?
- Does the DBMS force me to do this?

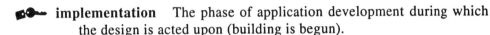 **implementation**   The phase of application development during which the design is acted upon (building is begun).

These four questions really span the spectrum of the way any feature is implemented by a DBMS. As Fig. 8-6 suggests, the most powerful implementation (the most relational) is one in which the DBMS takes complete control, in other words, *forces* the user to apply the feature. This ensures that any application (or data) always conforms to the model.

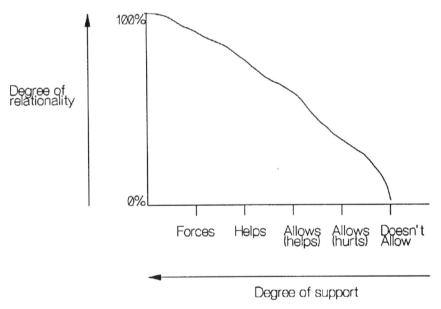

8-6   RDBMS support for relational features.

An implementation that helps the user take advantage of a feature is normally fairly powerful; helping a feature be used implies that the feature has been made simpler or easier to use. Any feature that is easy to use is more likely to be taken advantage of than one that is difficult to master. Somewhat less powerful is an implementation in which the DBMS simply allows the use of the feature; normally this level of support is provided through a programming language rather than through any interactive system. Finally, the least powerful implementation is one that the DBMS allows to happen (again, probably through a programming language) but doesn't optimize in any way. In this case, use of the feature slows down any application to an unacceptable speed and makes an application so difficult to use that it ensures failure.

In your own evaluation, you might want to use these questions to rank a DBMS. A DBMS receiving a rank of 4 supports a given feature more powerfully than one receiving a rank of 1 (see Table 8-1). Of course, no support for the feature would receive a 0.

Table 8-1 Example evaluation issues for support of relational operations by an RDBMS.

Feature	Type of support	Rank
Simple project	Query by example	4
Union of two tables	Command driven	2
Union of two tables	Query by example	4
Subtract one table from another	Menu driven	3
Join	Query by example	4

Assessing the importance of a feature

Note carefully the designations in Tables 8-2 through 8-4 that indicate the importance of each feature or class of features to relationality. A value of 5 is given to those features that are required to support a minimally relational system; these are the most important features. The lowest value, 1, is given to those rules that must be met in order to support the definition of fully relational. A value of 3 is given to those rules that must be met in order to support the definition of relationally complete. In effect, the lower the value, the less important the feature; conversely, the higher the value, the less relational a system need be to support it. For your evaluation purposes, you might want to develop a combined ranking that integrates the power of the DBMS support for a feature with the importance of that feature to the model.

Table 8-2 Features of the relational model regarding data structures.

Rule number	Description	Relative importance
RS–1	Information all found in tables, and nothing but tables	5
RS–2	No ordering of rows or columns	5
RS–3	No duplicate rows	5
RS–4	Information independent of site or equipment	5
RS–5	Three-level architecture of views, tables, and storage	5
RS–8	Each table has a primary key	5
RD–2	Logical and physical structures are separate	5
RD–3	There is a sharp distinction between performance issues and logical issues	5
RN–1 to RN–3	Names of domains, data types, relations, functions and columns must be distinct	3
RN–4	Table and column name always used in combination	5
RN–5 and RN–6	Relational operations not dependent on column names but on data	5
RN–7	Names of columns must not impair commutativity of operations	3
RN–8 to RN–11	Names of columns resulting from operations are inherited where possible	3
RN–12	Archived relations can have new names	3
RC–1	An on-line catalog providing all pertinent database information as a table	5
RC–2	DBMS must support concurrent users	3
RC–3 to RC–6	Domains, tables, and views are described in the catalog	5
RC–7 to RC–11	Integrity constraints, user-defined functions, security (authorization) information, and database statistics contained in the catalog	5
RV–1	Views are supported and defined in the catalog	5
RV–2 to RV–8	How views are to be managed by DBMS	5

Table 8-2 Continued.

Rule number	Description	Relative importance
RV–6	Different views are more or less updatabale	3
RP–1	Physical-data-storage techniques can be changed without affecting application	5
RP–2	Logical data independence; tables can be manipulated with operators without loss of information based on algorithm VU–1	5
RP–4 and RP–5	Location of data is independent of logical organization	3
RD–4 and RD–5	Applications independent from concurrency issues; long-term locks are not permitted	3
RD–6	No features are coupled together without clearly stated, logically defensible reasons	3
RD–7 to RD–16	Implications for designers of DBMS products	3

Table 8-3 Features of the relational model regarding data integrity.

Rule number	Description	Relative importance
RS–6	Domain is extended data type	1
RS–7	Column description includes domain and additional rules	1
RS–9	Appropriate views have primary keys	1
RS–10	Foreign-key identification as part of column description	1
RS–11 and 12	Domains and columns can be declared as composite	1
RS–13	Missing data indicated with a special mark	1
RS–14	All tables not stored by DBMS as one big combined table	1
RT–1	Values not compared unless they are based on the same domain	1
RT–2	Dates, times, and currency supported as data types; dates and times calculated, and current date and time available	1

Rule number	Description	Relative importance
RT–3	Users can define extended data types	1
RT–4 to RT–7	Date and time components can be manipulated individually by the DBMS, and can be coupled together when necessary	1
RT–8 and RT–9	Currency data types supported as extension of integer data type	1
RF–9 and FR–10	Function and arguments names supported as part of domain and column definitions	1
RN–13	Each integrity constraint must have a name	1
RM–14 to RM–20	Miscellaneous integrity constraints	1
RI–1 to RI–5	Integrity constraints are of five types: domain, field, entity, referential, and user-defined (business rules)	1
RI–6 to RI–22	How integrity issues are to be handled	1
RI–23 to RI–34	How user-defined integrity constraints are to be handled	1
RA–1	Authorization is granted rather than denied	1
RA–2 to RA–16	How the DBMS should grant or modify authorization; what operations can be authorized	1
RP–3	Integrity independence; application is unchanged when integrity rules change	1

Table 8-4 Features of the relational model regarding operations on data.

Rule number	Description	Relative importance
RD–1	No fundamental laws of mathematics are violated	3
RE–1 and RE–2	Commands to find values in a domain	3
RB–1	Cartesian product not an operator	3
RB–2	Project	5

Table 8-4 Continued.

Rule number	Description	Relative importance
RB–3 to RB–12	Restrict (select)	5
RB–13	Boolean extension of select	3
RB–14 to RB–23	Join	5
RB–24	Boolean extension of join	3
RB–25	Natural join	3
RB–26 to RB–28	Union, intersection, and difference	3
RB–29	Relational division	3
RB–30 to RB–37	Manipulative operators (assignment, insert, update, delete, cascading update, and delete)	3
RZ–1 to RZ–40	Advanced operators (includes extend, outer joins, and recursive join)	3
RN–14	Query can include an option for a name	3
RE–3 to RE–19	Commands for the DBA to create, rename, or alter domains, tables, and columns	3
RE–20	Delete duplicate rows	3
RE–21 and RE–22	Archive and restore commands	3
RQ–1 to RQ–13	Qualifiers for dealing with missing data	3
RJ–1 to RJ–14	Indicators for marking errors or problems in results of operations	3
RM–1	Each value is accessible through a combination of table name, primary key value, and column name	3
RM–2 to RM–5	Operations supported by four-valued, first-order predicate logic (at set level)	3

Rule number	Description	Relative importance
RM–6 and RM–7	Changes to database made in combination, and committed only when all changes are possible	3
RM–8 and RM–9	Some operations can occur dynamically without halting system; all can be executed interactively in programs, or in case of error	3
RM–10 to RM–13	What happens when operating on missing values	3
RZ–41 to RZ–44	Operations on partially normalized views and tables	3
RF–1	Supports at least Count, Sum, Average, Maximum, and Minimum functions	3
RF–2 to RF–10	How DBMS should handle functions	3
RL–1 to RL–17	Relational-command design principles for DBMS developers	3
RX–1 to RX–29	Support for distributed (multiple location) databases	3

Refer to Tables 8-2 through 8-4 for a rundown on each of the three areas of the model and their relative importance. The summary presented in these tables is not intended to convey the depth nor the detail of the different rules of the relational model. It is simply a rough overview of the model's features and is intended to be useful only as an introduction to some of the model's most pertinent features, and not as a technical analysis of its logic. This book does not intend to provide a measurement of the value of any specific relational DBMS on the market today; thus the case studies are not discussed here, nor are the designs adjusted to conform to or compensate for any RDBMS deficiencies.

Making other DBMS-driven adjustments to a design

Beyond their degree of adherence to the relational model, different RDBMS have specific features that can have an impact on a theoretical design.

Several of the most common differences between RDBMS products are addressed below. These potential restrictions most likely will be described in detail in your specific RDBMS manuals wherever the process of creating a table is described.

Naming conventions

In particular, naming conventions are almost always different between DBMS. Take a look at your DBMS rules for naming in two specific areas, specifically tables and fields.

A RDBMS may limit your ability to descriptively name either your tables or your fields. If (as is common) you are required to use short names, then abbreviating as necessary the meaningful, descriptive titles that you created during the design process is more useful than starting from scratch with meaningless names. Table 8-5 describes the abbreviated table and field names for case study 3, based on the assumption that table names are limited to 8 characters in length, while the field names are limited to 12 (no spaces allowed).

Table 8-5 Abbreviated table and field names for case study 3.

Design name	Abbreviated name
Animal	**Animal**
Animal ID*	AnimalID
Animal name	AnimalName
Date of birth	AnimalDOB
Cage number	Cage#
Ancestor	**Ancestor**
Animal ID*	AnimalID
Ancestor animal ID*	AncsAnimalID
Type of ancestor	AncsTypeID
Ancestor type	**AncsType**
Type of ancestor	AncsTypeID
Description of ancestor	AncsDescr
Cage	**Cage**
Cage number	Cage#
Cage name	CageName
Cage building	CageBldg
Cage row	CageRow
Cage level	CageLevel
Number of spaces total	TotSpace
Number of spaces available	AvailSpace

Selecting data types

The data type that you have specified for each field could need adjusting as well. Investigate the different data types supported by your RDBMS. Remember to select the data type that is most relevant to your expectations for the data in a field: one which helps you maintain the information content of a value whenever possible. Table 8-6 describes the adjusted data types for case study 2, based on the assumption that the selected RDBMS does not support a specific currency data type. This example might seem trivial, but you should be aware that the smallest change in data type can have powerful ramifications in a system that is up-and-running.

Table 8-6 Adjusting case study 2 data types for the RDBMS.

Field	Data type	Adjusted data type
Purchase order		
Purchase order number	N(4,0)	
Purchase order date	D	
Vendor ID	N(4,0)	
Vendor name	C(25)	
User name	C(40)	
Total purchase order amount	M(9)	N(7,2)
Purchase order date closed	D	
Buyer name	C(40)	
Item		
Item number	N(5,0)	
Quantity ordered	N(9,0)	
Price	M(6)	N(4,2)
Item description	C(15)	
Vendor		
Vendor ID	N(4,0)	
Vendor name	C(25)	
Street address	C(25)	
City	C(25)	
State	C(2)	
Zip code	C(10)	
Area code	C(3)	
Phone number	C(8)	
Purchase request		
Request number	N(4,0)	
Date requested	D	
Date updated	D	
User name	C(40)	

Limiting table widths

The process of relational design might have led you to define a table that has fifty columns, all of which are dependent on and describe the entity that is the intent of that table. From a practical standpoint, your RDBMS probably limits the number of columns in a table to some arbitrary maximum. On the other hand, the limitation for table width might be applied to the sum of the actual field widths. Some RDBMSs specify a maximum number of characters wide that a table can be. If this is an issue, consider separating the table into two tables related on a one-to-one basis.

Even though most RDBMSs do have a limit to table width, as a practical matter it is fairly unlikely that you'll run up against it. You'll be far more likely to encounter a practical limitation of performance that will force you to build smaller (narrower) tables (see chapter 9).

Modifying a design for nonrelational reasons

Finally, your design might need to be modified for reasons having little to do with your RDBMS and a lot to do with what is inherently reasonable. There are two areas that you should consider specifically:

- Ensuring security
- Choosing simplicity

Ensuring security

As chapter 7 described at length, the value of information exists as a continuum. Some information is useful and provides decision-making help; some is less useful and its benefit might not be immediately obvious. The integrity of the data helps to place it on the continuum at a higher or lower position (can I depend on it to be accurate or not?).

Beyond the integrity of the data, which relates in large part to how you manage the translation process (from information to data), information has its own inherent value. Some information is simply more important than other information. For example, you can probably do business if you don't know the name of a client's wife, but you'll undoubtedly lose your client if you don't know his (the client's) name.

In addition to the relative value of information, but somewhat related to it, is the issue of the information's sensitivity. The *sensitivity* of information is a qualitative assessment that describes how secret it is. Secrecy is more an issue in some businesses than in others, and thus security is more important in some applications than in others. *Security* is simply the way an application enforces the need for secrecy. If an application manages sensitive information, security must be built into the system.

---

data sensitivity   A qualitative assessment of data that describes how secret it is.

Security can be applied at several levels within a business system. Incidentally, it is at issue with the business system overall, not simply with an application, because the behavior of the users will have a direct impact on the way any security is enforced. In any case, the actual mechanism for creating a secure application (in the appropriate places) varies from RDBMS to RDBMS. However, many RDBMSs allow an application to apply security at a table level, because this is where you might consider adjusting your design to this kind of requirement.

Specifically, if your application utilizes sensitive information, you might want to consider isolating it in a table separate from those you've already defined. Capturing all the information that requires security in a single table can ease the process of building a security mechanism as part of your application. The "secure" table can be built in a one-to-one relationship with the already defined, less sensitive table from which the data came (see Fig. 8-7). This ensures that the separation will have no impact on your ability to access the information in exactly the same way as you could before the separation.

Member table

ID	Name	Height	Build	Age
2	Mark	Tall	Muscular	Youthful
1	Mark	Short	Thin	Teenager
3	Margaret	Tall	Thin	Youthful

Weight table

ID	Weight
1	160
2	210
3	140

(protected)

8-7 Sensitive data can be isolated into separate database tables.

Choosing simplicity

Above and beyond any other issue, considering how reasonable your relational design is an important step. Regardless of how easy to use an RDBMS might be, using it to manage multiple tables is never as easy as using it to manage one table. Anathema to the relational model though it might be, the simplest design could in fact be the best, and a single table can be more appropriate than multiple tables. All the relational arguments aside, a single table is often easier to think about, and thus easier to use, than even the most carefully designed multitable system. Besides, some users just like the sense that they can wrap their arms around the entire set of data at one time, without having to go through any relational hoops first.

This issue is something to consider at the end, not at the beginning, of a database design process, because only at this point can you make a good assessment of what the needs of the business system might be. A small number of records and relatively simple information suggest that use of a single table will not adversely affect the integrity of the data, nor the ultimate functionality of any application that uses it.

A design also might be modified if there are output requirements that cannot be met directly by a fully relational design. Before taking a look at this issue, it is important to touch briefly on some fundamentals of output design, specifically as they relate to reporting.

Considering database output

From the beginning of this database design process, it has been stressed that the way you logically store your data and the techniques you employ to use it probably will vary dramatically. The issues involved are so different: as a user who works directly with creating input and evaluating output, you need to be able to use the information that is available to you without going through a lot of hoops before you can understand it; as a computer system, the RDBMS needs to have specific and secure access to data, which is provided through the relational database design. The foregoing is obvious as a quick summary, but it reflects the fundamental purpose for a database design (at any level).

In essence, the rules you apply to information differs from those you apply to data. Thus, when you think about data, you think about database design; but when you think about information output, you think about output design (reports, graphs, etc.).

What output is

Output is both a noun and a verb. In different contexts, it describes either the data being extracted from a DBMS (the report in my hand is output) or the process of data extraction itself (I am outputting this report). For the purposes of this discussion, output is used as a noun, and *output design* refers to the design process that results in a report or graph.

By now, when you think about database design you'll probably have a sense of great order: there are rules to follow and guidelines to meet, and there are methodologies that have been developed in order to facilitate the process. However, when you think about report design, you probably have a much more limited sense of the process. Output is controlled traditionally by the needs of the user, and by nature (at least in the PC world) is pretty free-form. In fact, one of the driving forces toward PCs (away from mainframe and minicomputer systems) has always been the PC's ability to put reporting (output) power in the hands of users. The number of options—how they'll look, what they'll do—has always been limited only by the numbers of businesses and individuals who can dream them up.

In essence, output design is a relatively free-form creation of the frame for information of value. After all, output should be a delivery system for that information. One of the most important things to recognize about output design is that how the information is delivered (the appearance of the output—the data selected, organization, and overall look) is a crucial element in the design. Formats not only make users/readers more comfortable during a learning curve, but they also actually can have an impact on, or even slant, the information given. This is particularly true in the case of a graph, which is by nature a powerful decision-making tool. Graphs almost always display highly summarized data, and thus are more an argument about the data than a presentation of the data itself.

An overview of the output-design process

The output-design process is much like a condensed version of the application-design process. Just as application development goes through the identification of requirements, design, building, testing, installation, training, and evaluation phases (as described earlier in Fig. 2-1), so the development of output goes through similar steps. The process generally covers the following steps:

1. Identifying the purpose of the output.
2. Determining the data requirements.
3. Organizing the output.
4. Detailing the appearance.

Just as the database design process involves the requirements identification and design phases of application development, so the output-design process involves the same phases. Once the design has been created, you can take it and, using your specific RDBMS, build, test, install, train users, and evaluate it. Thus, these first three steps are independent of the RDBMS; you can apply these techniques to output design regardless of the RDBMS you use.

Identifying the purpose for the output

The first question you must ask is why I need this output? Because need normally drives your development, the answer to the question probably is close at hand. However, sometimes in the application development process, you might think that you have a need for a report or a graph of some sort, although you've never answered the question of why. If you cannot document (and verify) this need, you shouldn't be spending the time to pursue a solution to it.

You also need to get beyond the simple, probably general answer to why you need the output. Dig deeper to figure out specifically what you intend to do with the output. Will you be making a decision based on what you see in the report? Will you be asking for a raise based on the graph you have prepared? Will you be cutting off the credit of a customer based on the report? The purpose should be more specific than a general need to know. In fact, the very best reports and graphs work because they answer the most specific kind of question: they meet the requirement because it has been defined so exactly.

In fact, this detailed description of your purpose shouldn't just identify the format of the output; it should define it. In other words, you should select the output format (report or graph, and even the type of report or graph) based on the requirements, not the other way around. Different purposes are better served through a report output with its textual display, which can integrate a number of different values than a graphic display, which can focus attention only on a very few, directly related values.

However, what is a "good" report or graph? What differentiates it in quality from other output? One definition could focus on the fact that a good output is one that gives you the information you need and only the information you need. In fact, one of the worst things that a report or graph can do is tell you too much. Too much information will always fog the issue (and unless that is your specific goal, you'd be better off avoiding the fog). As Fig. 8-8 suggests, the best, or ideal, output, normally will be focused on its purpose (often indicated in the report title or graph heading) and will include only the data necessary to achieve its purpose. Relationships that you need to highlight to convey the information are marked clearly and even set apart in some way, if through nothing else than by being juxtaposed one next to the other. This makes for an unclut-

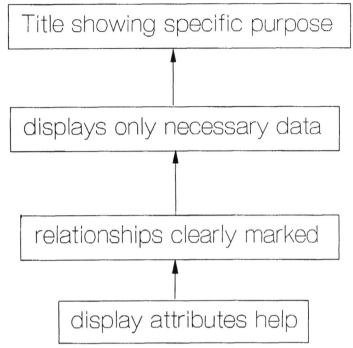

Title showing specific purpose

↑

displays only necessary data

↑

relationships clearly marked

↑

display attributes help

8-8 An ideal output will follow four specific guidelines.

tered, simple, usually short output, and in the case of a graph, allows it to be understandable.

Many applications use just a few, general-purpose reports or graphs to convey all the information of value in the system. You should consider whether this is truly cost-effective. If you can more specifically identify how the report or graph will be used, you can customize each output to its intended need, creating a different report or graph for each variation. This will reduce dramatically the time it takes to use the report—to achieve its intended purpose.

Determining the data requirements

Once the purpose specifically has been identified, you can proceed by focusing on what data is necessary to convey the intended information. The two aspects to consider are what table/fields contain the data and what records contain the data.

Remember that data in a relational database always is referenced by a combination of column and row position. Each value is found in the intersection of a column and row, and thus always is used by accessing it through that combination. So in order to figure out what data needs to be used for a particular output, you need to look at both sides of the question.

What table/fields contain the data   This is the normal focus of a report design, because the implementation of a design in any RDBMS requires the fields to be specified. If you need to figure out who in your Family database owns a blue car in order to send them a "Blue Car Owner's Newsletter," you'll need to know the name of that person and his or her address; you might also want to know what make and model of blue car it is that they own. So on your report design you'll need to specify name and address in some way. Figure 8-9 displays a report design relevant to this point.

If the fields you need are found in more than one table, you must consider whether or not the tables are related in the database design. If they are (and if your DBMS is an RDBMS, which of course it should be) you should be able to rely on the RDBMS to provide you with a means to use multiple tables' fields in a single output. This might involve creating a multiple-table report design, or creating some kind of query to combine the data into a single table before attempting to design the report or graph output.

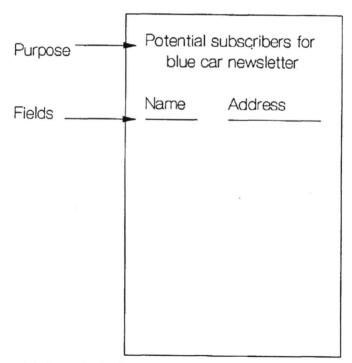

8-9 A report design under development.

What records contain the data In addition to the table/field specification, you need to consider whether or not you want to see every value in the table or tables, or if your output's purpose focuses on a specific selection of values. If there is a specific selection (or subset) required, make sure you indicate it in the report design (see Fig. 8-10). Again, different RDBMS implement selection of records differently, but this is an important technique for making a report or graph better—or more usable—reducing the amount of information shown.

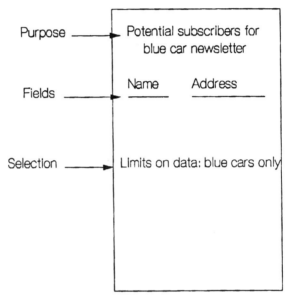

8-10 Documenting the record specifications.

In fact, this is one area in which graphs can be more powerful than reports; graphs tend to demand reduction of information, or fewer rather than more records for display. It is usually very obvious what a graph's purpose is: every report should have that same level of focus.

Organizing the output

It is interesting to note that a well-focused graph is not usually described as organized. Because the information to be conveyed is presented in a format that reduces the pertinent facts to their most basic, you ordinarily don't look at the use of a graph as sequential, but as "one shot." In other words, you should be able to understand what the graph is saying within moments of looking at it. You ordinarily don't break a graph down into ordered, sequential facts. Even if there are several issues being covered, a graph usually allows you to review them as you need, partially because it is encompassed within a single image, usually on a single page. However, this is also partly true because a graph already has selected the pertinent data for you and shows you only that. Don't be misled. Graphs must be organized, but at a different (lower) level. A graph's organization usually focuses on the types of descriptive elements used, the graph values selected, and the order these appear on the axes or in the legend.

Reports, on the other hand, tend to regard organization as crucial. When you look at a report, you expect to be led through the information in some kind of ordered fashion; if you need to find something specific within the body of the report, you expect to be able to do so quite readily. This kind of hand-holding is necessary because traditionally reports tend to tell you everything you ever wanted to know, and everything you never cared about, to begin with. Thus, the very best kind of organization comes through the identification of the purpose of the report. If the purpose is focused, the data will be restricted, and the need for organization will be minimized.

This said, the order in which data appears in a report is crucial and must be carefully planned. Order is provided in a report through some kind of sorting mechanism; a sort usually is based on a data value, and thus in your report design you must specify a sort by identifying which field contains that data value.

---

sort   The arrangement of values into a specified order, usually following the ASCII keycode order.

Many reports have so much data included that a single sort does not provide adequate organization. Thus, multiple sorts (called *sort levels* or sometimes *breaks*) can be used. Multiple sorts usually are implemented using a technique called *nesting*, wherein the first sort happens first, then within the first sorted group the second sort takes place. These are sort levels because the first sort takes precedence over the second, which takes precedence over the third, etc.

Sorting by a value results in what is known as a *grouping* of data. For example, if you are sorting a text field you'll probably be expecting to see it in alphabetic order, and thus all the A's will be together, then the B's, then the C's, and so on. If the field you were sorting contained only a single letter (A or B or X or Z, for example), the sort would result in four groups of records: the A's would be together, the B's next, the X's next, and then the Z's. A group is a collection of records (such as each of these

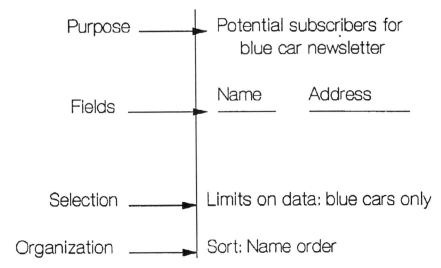

8-11 Documenting the report organization.

four) that all share a same quality, in this case, the same value in the sort-ed field.

If your report's purpose requires that you evaluate a variety of infor-mation, you will need to organize it adequately to meet that purpose, and your design will need to reflect that organization (see Fig. 8-11).

Detailing the appearance

Although the features of an output that identify its appearance might seem trivial, they often have a dramatic impact on how the output is received, and whether it is used to achieve its intended purpose. These features—which can include the fonts, the spacing, the colors or patterns on a graph—won't affect the essence of what is communicated, but they will help focus the user's attention on the priorities that you establish. You can look at these kind of decisions as being an extension of the organi-zation of the output. You are attempting essentially to control what the user looks at first (what is most important?), and in so doing to affect their overall perception of the information. You can detail these choices in an output specification, or you can leave them to the RDBMS, which ordi-narily uses a set of default values to handle these kinds of issues.

Summary

In this chapter, you took a first look at applying reality to a decidedly the-oretical design. In particular, you learned that:

- It is nearly impossible to avoid choosing practice over theory, because there are elements you must consider in implementing a design that any current RDBMS does not manage for you.
- Relationality is a spectrum spanning nonrelational (tabular) DBMS through fully relational DBMS (which don't exist today).
- You can assess your DBMS by reviewing the summarized rules and evaluating a combination of factors: how well your DBMS supports the feature, and how important that feature is.
- There are other issues to consider that most DBMSs deal with in different ways. Specifically, nonrelational issues that your choice of RDBMS will affect include naming conventions, selection of data types, and limits on table width.
- You need to consider adjusting a relational database design for nonrelational reasons, including the need for security for your information, and a desire for simplicity.
- You need to consider how your database design will be implemented through particular output, including reports and graphs.
- Designing output is like a condensed version of database design: you must focus on the end result first: "Why do I need this output?"

9
CHAPTER

Evaluating application performance

You have designed your application, and specifically your database, to perform an accurate translation of your information to the computer-managed data. Similarly, you've put the mechanisms in place (table links) that enable your application to recreate your information from the data being stored. You've analyzed how the design might need to be modified based on the specific parameters of your computer environment, in particular, the relational database management system that you have chosen. However, these considerations fail to address a critical aspect of your goal: for information to be information of value, it not only must be accurate but timely.

What makes information timely?

Timely is a term that can mean different things in different contexts. Information on a report might be timely if it reflects what happened last week; information on a graph might be timely if it shows today's sales; information that you need to modify through an application might be timely only if it reflects what is known—up to the minute. Although the term *performance* often is used to describe how quickly a task is accomplished (interchangeably with the term *speed*), performance is more accurately a measure of timeliness. While speed is an objective measure of the time it takes to accomplish a task (five seconds per task, 30 minutes per task, etc.), performance is more subjective, measured relative to the timeliness requirement of the given situation. Thus, an application might run at high speed (a task happens quickly) but have inadequate performance (it doesn't happen quickly enough).

 speed   How fast a given task can be accomplished in an application.

In evaluating the performance of an application, you must consider what is timely: how quickly do you need a task to occur in order for the information to retain its value? Once these performance requirements have been established, you can evaluate the speed of the different system components to determine which areas need enhancement.

Considering real-time

One of the major advantages of creating a computer-based application is that it can manage large quantities of data, but in some respects an even greater advantage is such a system's ability to manage these quantities in real-time. *Real-time* refers to the closeness of the connection between what is happening in the real world and what is going on in the database. A real-time application will maintain a close match between the two; a change in the real world will be reflected immediately in the database. Analysis done with real-time data is as accurate as possible, because it reflects what is happening now, not what happened yesterday or last week or last month.

 real-time   A close connection between what is happening in the real world and what is going on in the database.

The term immediately isn't a very good way to describe the time it takes an application to reflect an activity in the real world, because there is an actual span of time involved. Ordinarily, an application is real-time only when users collect the necessary information and enter it into the application at the same time. In that case, the collection and entry/modification of the information support each other, and the factor that controls the speed of the system is the user (how quickly she can collect the information) and not the application.

Thus, performance is a cumulative measurement that is affected by both the application's speed and the speed of the user.

Assessing your performance expectations

Practically speaking, it might be tough to figure out how fast you need a task to occur, particularly if you are converting from a manual system that probably has a very different performance expectation. Because performance is hard to evaluate and even harder to specify, many application designers ignore the issue until after an application is in place. If there are complaints that the application runs too slowly, then these considerations suddenly apply. However, reacting after the fact rarely yields a satisfactory solution. Assessing performance after the fact could even force you to reconsider database design issues that more appropriately are evaluated right up front.

Performance specification usually involves coming up with a maximum time for each task. For example, my daily sales report must run in under 15 minutes; my monthly sales report must run in two hours or less; data entry of one sales transaction must take no longer than three minutes. If the application performs in under that maximum time, great, but if it comes in above the maximum (it takes longer than specified), something must be done. The basic problem is that an application that is too slow won't get used, remembering that "too slow" can be on the user's side ("I don't know how to make this work and I don't have the time to figure it out") or on the application side ("I have to wait forever for the report to print; I can do it faster manually").

This issue follows the concept of a bottleneck: which component is slowing you down? Which component, if enhanced, will measurably affect the performance? The bottom line is that age-old equation: time equals money. It costs money to buy time; in this case, it costs money to enhance an application's performance. Your goal in assessing the value of that enhancement is to do the best job of leveraging any dollars you must invest (see chapter 10 for a more detailed discussion). This means that you should pay to speed up an application only in the areas in which you will gain the most from enhanced performance. If a user is the primary bottleneck, work at enhancing the user's speed (the basic technique: training!). However, if the application is the bottleneck, look at the pieces of the application that you can enhance.

So, to do your own application analysis, you need to take a look at several issues. First, where will performance be a concern (where are the bottlenecks)? Second, what are the factors that will influence that performance?

Note that the goal at this point in the database design process is not to focus on the user side of the system (this is more appropriately reserved for a thorough application-design discussion). Instead, you need to focus on the database side, and to consider specifically where modifying the database design will help and where it could hinder performance.

Figuring out the bottlenecks

Each kind of input and output task varies in complexity, at least from the application's standpoint (the goal for the user, of course, is to find even the most complex tasks easy to perform). In general (just like in a manual system), the more complex a task, the more time it takes. Table 9-1 lists the categories of application tasks described in chapter 2, reordered based on relative speed. Note that Table 9-1 is only a very rough ordering of the relative speeds of these tasks. Each RDBMS uses different implementation techniques, and thus could yield markedly different speeds in these areas that could affect the relative speed order in which the tasks would be completed. This table also expands the list somewhat, adding some new subcategories to those tasks; most RDBMSs differentiate between tasks involving one table and tasks involving multiple tables. Obviously, multitable tasks will be common in relational applications, but you will pay a price for that functionality in speed. Figure 9-1 provides a rough comparison of how that price varies for different tasks, all other performance-impacting factors being equal.

Before you specifically address how these issues will affect your database design, you need to consider what factors influence speed in

Table 9-1 Application input/output ordered by speed.

Task	Relative speed
Answer single-table question	Fast
Single-table data entry	Fast
Single-table data modification	Fairly fast
Generate single-table report	Fair
Perform single-table analysis	Fair
Multitable data entry	Fair
Multitable data modification	Fairly slow
Answer two-table question	Fairly slow
Generate graph	Fairly slow
Generate multitable report	Slow
Answer multitable question	Slow

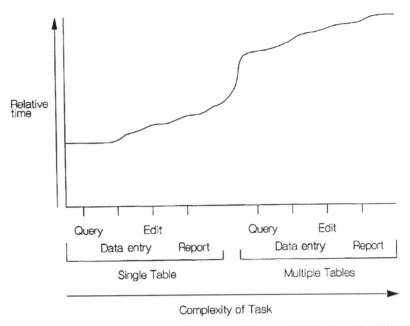

Complexity of Task

9-1 Multitable input and output tasks take substantially more time than single-table tasks.

general. If each of your application tasks meet your performance goals, no redesign of your database might be necessary.

Understanding PC speed

To understand why an application slows where it does, you need a sense of the basic components of a PC. Consider this an extremely rough overview of which PC components contribute to making a task occur and which usually affect how fast or slow the task occurs. There are many more highly technical books available on these topics; this is by no means a comprehensive discussion.

You need to start with a brief review of the elements of a PC. Figure 9-2 graphically describes the basic categories: hardware, and software. These components work together to accomplish any task (relative costs are discussed briefly in chapter 9).

Software components

Software provides the basic set of instructions which you, or your application, use to accomplish a task. If your task involves data, and specifically involves data in relational tables, your software likely will be a relational DBMS. Your RDBMS software in turn works with the operating

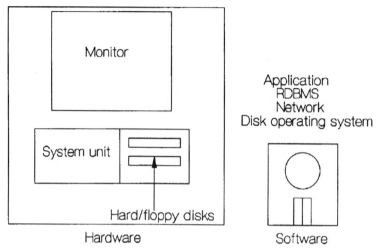

Application
RDBMS
Network
Disk operating system

Hardware

Software

9-2 Elements of a PC.

system (on a PC, this is most commonly DOS) to manipulate the various hardware components of the PC. Your RDBMS also must work with any *network operating system*, an additional "layer" of software that is required for linking multiple PCs together in a network, if your application needs to use data on a PC that is not your own.

Different RDBMSs accomplish the same task at different speeds, because the mechanism each uses is likely to be different. Any software review that compares different RDBMSs is likely to compare speeds to perform the same task (see Miller, ed., 1991). You just need to be aware that your choice of DBMS affects how quickly your application tasks are accomplished.

Hardware components

The hardware components that have a direct and measurable impact on speed fall into three areas. Each of these is a resource with a finite limit:

- Disk drive
- Memory
- Processor

The disk drive(s) in your computer are used to store data. *Disk speed* is a measure of how quickly data can be read from or written to it. When an application needs to use data, it first must find it on the disk and then make it available to use (*read* it). The faster the disk speed, the faster that data can be retrieved, and the faster your task that needs the data can be completed. In general, any task that must use data from disk storage will be slower than one that doesn't; because database applications by definition use data (and usually lots of it), they also tend to do a lot of disk reads and writes. This is one reason why PC database application developers are said to be "power users"; database applications often demand all the resources they can get.

 disk storage   Magnetic media used to store data permanently.

Memory is the hardware area that provides a temporary holding and manipulation space for all the things the computer needs to do. Memory (more specifically random access memory, or *RAM*) is similar to the top of your desk: it is where you bring things together, review, write, summarize, and generally get things done, with your information. For a computer to do anything, to perform a calculation or help you draw any conclusions, or even to allow you to look at the data that is stored out there on the disk, the data must be available in memory. Thus, the read and write functions that the disk performs are more specifically reads and writes from the disk into memory, where you can see and work with the data.

 memory (or RAM)   Random access memory, used temporarily to store and process data.

In general, the more memory you have available on your PC, the faster things will work. This is because displaying or manipulating data already in memory is substantially faster than having to go out and retrieve it off of a disk (even the fastest disks). In fact, purchasing memory can be the cheapest way to improve performance across the board, at least if you have an RDBMS that is able to take advantage of it (see chapter 10).

The *processor* is the hardware component that provides the capability actually to do things to the data. When you buy a PC, the first question asked (even before the manufacturer's name) is what "kind" you're buying—a PC, an XT, an AT/286, a 386, a 386SX, or a 486—each of these refers to the type of processor that the PC uses. The more powerful and sophisticated processors are those most recently developed; as a bottom line a 486 is faster than a 386, which is faster than a 386SX, which is faster than a 286/AT, etc. Again, speed is almost always what you're paying for when you purchase a more expensive machine.

A discussion of which kind of machine will give you the best performance for dollars spent is again outside of the scope of the book. However, be aware that database applications in general push all available hardware resources to their limits. Today's RDBMSs are designed to run on faster hardware; no matter what you do to maximize performance through your database design, you might never get the performance you require from an RDBMS application without investing in hardware at the 286/AT level or above.

Modifying a design for performance reasons

Before you even consider modifying a database design in order to make an application work faster, take special note: relational theory is intended to provide the best solution to the needs of a relational database system *in most circumstances*. Most of the situations under which you might decide to modify a design are specific to the current form of an application. Beware, however, that in optimizing your design for a certain task or set of tasks you don't reduce the flexibility and power inherent in a truly relational database. You might not think you need flexibility, but recall the discussion in chapter 2 about growth; even if you don't need to do some particular task today, there might be a good chance that you'll need to do it tomorrow. If in optimizing for today you've reduced your options for tomorrow, you might not be making a good buy.

All this considered, there are three major areas in which a relational database design might need modification in order to meet or enhance minimum performance requirements.

- Building indexes
- Minimizing the width of the primary tables
- Recombining tables for speed

Building indexes

In general, the slowest tasks are those that manipulate the largest amounts of data. However, what are these tasks, and how can you make them faster? The tasks most related to these issues are:

1. Reports
2. Queries
3. Sorting

You need to revisit the concept of a primary key just for a moment. Recall that the way most RDBMSs implement a primary key is through the building of an index, a machine-readable file that keeps track of each primary key value and where it actually is located in the table. The goal for a primary index is to make sure that each value in the table is unique, but a benefit of that index is that rows in the table can be obtained much more quickly than before (pre-index).

 primary key   The field or fields used as the identifier for each record in a table.

Most RDBMSs support the use of additional indexes that can be built simply for the purpose of speeding up the tasks in an application. This kind of index, called a *secondary index* because it is built on a nonprimary key field, acts just like a primary index, except that it doesn't force values to be unique. A secondary index records the values in a specific field (the indexed field), keeping them in order (just like a primary index does), and keeps track of where each of these values is located in the table itself, too. So building a secondary index on a field that will be used to get at data in a table is a good way immediately to speed up tasks that use that table in this way. An index really helps only when you are looking to find a value in that field of the table (in performing a search); searches commonly are performed either in answer to a query (question) or as part of the preparation or organization of data for a report.

 secondary index   An index built on a nonprimary key field.

The down side to an index has to do with keeping it current. Although a primary index is always up-to-date (it has to be in order to control the uniqueness of the values), a secondary index might or might not reflect the current values in the table. Most RDBMSs allow you to specify whether a secondary index will be kept up-to-date like a primary index (this is called a *maintained* index). In the alternative, you usually can specify that an index should be kept in a nonmaintained state, at least until you need to use it; in this case the updating of the secondary index occurs when the DBMS detects that it is needed (normally during a query or reporting session). The real trade-off here is whether you want the best performance during your data maintenance sessions, in which case you'll choose nonmaintained indexing, because that way no time is devoted to secondary index maintenance during the data entry or edit session; or whether you'd rather have the speed during a query or reporting session, in which case you'll have to live with it if the data maintenance process takes a little longer.

Analyzing your field usage

Your database design should specify which fields should be indexed, but how do you determine this? You need to build a field usage matrix that you can use in this evaluation and in considering other issues as well. The basic technique is to build a two-dimensional structure (a table!) that will contain one dimension for each task and one dimension for each table/field combination in your database (see Fig. 9-3, which describes a matrix for case study 3). Whether you select rows or columns for each dimension depends on how many tasks the application will perform relative to how many fields there are in the application. The fewer of the two should be in the column "dimension." Once you've created the matrix, go through your lists of input and output tasks, and place a checkmark in the column(s) that are being used in that task. Place a special mark (an asterisk or check) in that column or columns that describe a field that is used specifically to direct that task (see Fig. 9-4). Here "specifically direct" refers to a field value being used in a search or linking process.

Once you've created this matrix, it should be easy to see which fields should be indexed. Add that designation to your database design with a symbol (like a bullet) placed next to the field name in your list of tables and fields (see Table 9-2).

Task/field matrix	Print animal list	Print genealogy	Print cage space list	Enter new births	Modify animal records	Display animal data	Maintain cage data
Animal ID							
Animal Name							
Date of Birth							
Cage #							
Ancestor Animal ID							
Type of Ancestor							
Description of Ancestor							
Cage Name							
Cage Building							
Cage Row							
Cage Level							
Total Spaces							
Available Spaces							

9-3 Input/output tasks and field matrix.

Task/field matrix

	Print animal list	Print genealogy	Print cage space list	Enter new births	Modify animal records	Display animal data	Maintain cage data
Animal ID	✓			✓		✓	
Animal Name	✓	✓		✓	✓	✓	
Date of Birth	✓			✓		✓	
Cage #							
Ancestor Animal ID		✓		✓		✓	
Type of Ancestor				✓		✓	
Description of Ancestor		✓					
Cage Name	✓		✓			✓	✓
Cage Building			✓				✓
Cage Row			✓				✓
Cage Level			✓				✓
Total Spaces							✓
Available Spaces			✓				✓

9-4 Input/output tasks and field usage.

Table 9-2 Tables and fields for case study 3
including critical-link indicators.

Table	Field
Animal	Animal ID*
	Animal Name++
	Date of birth
	Cage number
Ancestor	Animal ID*
	Ancestor animal ID*
	Type of ancestor
Ancestor type	Type of ancestor*
	Description of ancestor
Cage	Cage number*
	Cage name
	Cage building++
	Cage row++
	Cage level++
	Number of spaces total
	Number of spaces available++

++Secondary index recommended

181

Even if the appropriate fields have secondary indexes, your application still might not meet your performance expectations. So what other design areas should you look at?

Minimizing the width of the primary tables

In general, relational DBMS are intended to perform their best (i.e., fastest) when manipulating tables that have few columns and lots of rows. Narrow (fewer than 20 columns) is in almost every case better than wide, at least from a performance standpoint. After all, a theoretically sound relational database usually consists of many tables with relatively few columns in each.

For this reason you might want to consider reducing the size of the tables you work with most frequently. If you ask questions about or produce reports on the information in a table that is relatively wide, you might consider dividing your data into most-frequently-used and less-frequently-used categories. You can create easily a separate table with a one-to-one relationship to the first table, keeping both sets of data available at the same time through a link. You wouldn't see any functional difference in your application, that is, things would work exactly the same way. However, you would notice a substantial improvement in performance when you need to do those tasks that use only one (narrower) table's data.

To make this kind of evaluation, look at your task/field matrix. You'll be able to see graphically which fields fall into the most-frequently-used category, and which don't.

Recombining tables for speed

On the other side of the fence, you should be aware that having more tables will exact a different price. Every time you must access data from multiple tables at the same time, you will pay, simply because multitable tasks always take longer than those involving a single table. The question is whether that price is worth it. Remember, theoretically at least, the isolation of fields and tables is a good thing, even a requirement in many cases. Even in practice, it is usually advantageous. However, in some situations, you might have a need to recombine fields that describe different entities into a single table—a relational no-no—because if you don't, the performance price you pay every time you need the combination is just too high. So how do you assess whether to change your design? Which price is worth paying?

Ask yourself the following questions about how you will actually use your application:

- Do I ever deal with these entities separately?
- How frequently do I take advantage of a particular link?

Although two entities might be separate in theory, if in practice you always use them together, theory might just be wrong.

Take another look at your task/field matrix. Are the same tables always used in combination, or more specifically, is there ever a situation in which a table is used independently? If not, you might want to consider combining it with its *master*, the table with which it is always used. Even if you do use a table separately on occasion, your overwhelming usage of it in combination with another table (particularly if those combination usages are in the context of queries or reports) might be incentive enough for recombining them.

Summary

This chapter has addressed performance issues associated with an application. In particular, you have looked in detail at various aspects of information, including:

- Information of value must be timely, or it loses its value.

- Real-time applications are those that place a priority on being consistent with what is happening in the real world.

- You can figure out what you expect from an application's performance by evaluating the maximum time you'll allow a task to take before the application loses its value—before your users refuse to use it.

- The bottlenecks in an application's speed fall into a few specific categories, including software and hardware components.

- It is possible and even, under some circumstances, advisable, to modify a database design for performance reasons. In particular, you will want to evaluate building indexes, minimizing the width of your primary tables, and recombining your tables in order to enhance your application's speed.

10
CHAPTER

Evaluating the cost of a database

Your theoretical design already has changed shape; the impact of reality frequently forces modifications despite the requirements of theory. You've had to evaluate several implementation issues, including how your RDBMS actually works and under what circumstances—and all this before even getting started with the implementation!

The considerations you will address in this chapter might come last in the process as laid out in this book, but they probably will come first in your business. Every choice you make about an application involves the issue of money, because every choice you make in your business concerns that resource. Cost hits you everywhere, from the biggest picture (what's my bottom line with this application?) to the smallest detail (should I add one more field to my database design?). Even those issues that involve nothing more than your time involve cost; after all, time is money.

Throughout the design process you have deferred cost concerns to this chapter. The process of figuring out how much an application will cost and determining what the benefits of buying it will be is called *cost justification*. There are a number of formal methodologies that you can work through to develop extensive and detailed documentation about each aspect of the application-development process; it certainly is not the intent of this chapter to address the issue at that level. Instead, this general overview is intended to make you aware of the major cost areas and help you assess which of those might apply in your situation, and to what degree. It is not intended to balance them against the benefits you specifically will experience, although that evaluation is implicit in every cost decision you must make.

Identifying the cost components

First, you need to consider the two areas in which the costs of an application must be considered:

- Start-up costs
- Maintenance costs

It is all too common to look closely at the costs involved in developing and implementing an application, but ignore the longer term (and often more substantial) costs of operating it. This happens in large part because the start-up costs are heavily out-of-pocket; you can easily see any new equipment, new staffing, and consultant involvement as one big package. However, the costs an application will cause you to incur over time are also substantial; in fact, the biggest cause of application failure is a lack of planning about long-term issues, including maintenance and enhancement costs.

The costs involved in an application fall into two categories, which, as you might expect, are the same two categories that make up the application itself: users and application. You must consider both aspects; don't fall into the trap of ignoring the costs associated with the users. Although this book is focused on the database design issues involved in building an application (the computerized side of the equation), the user development/support issues are just as crucial, and unfortunately might be ignored more frequently.

You can break the costs down further into two additional categories: out-of-pocket and time. In most businesses, out-of-pocket expenses make it directly into the accounting system and demand thorough cost justification and explanation. However, unless they are associated with (and billed by) a consultant, time costs often are hidden. This fact represents a real failure in cost assessment (and justification), because in many cases the efficiency of business operations is involved directly in the push for new application development.

In addition, many businesses will implement a new application with the expectation that (over time) it will reduce the cost of doing business. The expectation is that the new application will make the users more efficient, thus allowing them to get more accomplished faster, thus (potentially) reducing the need for certain kinds of personnel. This attitude represents a common fear of many workers (particularly of PC-based systems), and might be responsible (at least partially) for the substantial resistance many users experience when beginning work with a new application (MIT 1990).

Interestingly enough, newly computer-based applications rarely, if ever, result in a reduction of staff. Much more commonly, the efficiencies engendered by a new application will provide the "breathing room" necessary to support business growth. This might not be possible immediately, because users will experience a learning curve with any new system; besides, any time freed up as the result of a new application is more than likely immediately to be absorbed by new tasks that only make themselves known once the system is underway. However, in the long term, computerized applications make it possible for a business to grow and be competitive in a business world that is increasingly computer dependent.

Start-up costs

The costs involved in getting a new application up and running are tied directly to the application-development process. To begin the cost evaluation, you first need to revisit the application life cycle discussed in chapter 1. You probably want to define further the term *start-up* as that part of the process associated with the first time through the cycle. You could consider the second time around as part of the ongoing costs of system maintenance.

In general, application-design costs should represent 30%–35% of the overall application-development costs (see Fig. 10-1). This reflects the relative time differential between the various phases of development. If the time/cost percentage is much less than that, you'll probably experience an immediate need for redesign.

Estimating disk storage requirements

Hardware costs must include an assessment of the disk storage capabilities an application will require. Making this kind of assessment might be difficult, particularly so for a newly computerized application. It is important, however, to come up with at least a rough "guesstimate." Not allocating enough disk space to an application obviously will affect your ability to store additional data, but less obviously likely will affect the ability of your application to perform its tasks and to get things done. Most RDBMSs have hidden disk storage requirements, hidden because they usually are undocumented, but nonetheless required. An area of the disk often is used for scratch or temporary tables used by the RDBMS when executing a process such as a query or preparing a report. These hidden requirements might be up to twice the size of the table that is being manipulated, for an additional requirement of 20%–25% more disk space across the entire application, depending on the size of the tables themselves and the kind of processing your application must do.

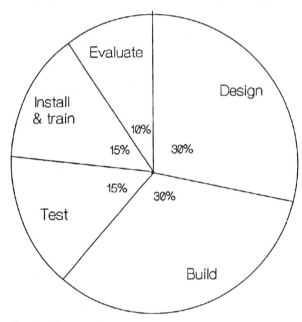

10-1   Application-development time.

In general, you can estimate the disk storage space required by figuring out the width of each table (adding up all the column widths) and multiplying the width by the number of records you anticipate locating in the table. A table to contain clients, for example, would be fairly easy to estimate; the rate with which you add new clients might be fairly low, and thus once you guess at the table size, you'll probably be fairly close for an extended period of time. On the other hand, the tables that contain daily business transactions—sales, appointments, contacts, etc.—are likely to grow much more quickly. If you estimate that the history you intend to keep immediately available in the system will cover six months, and you do 1000 sales per month, you can estimate that six months' worth of records will total 6000 records. If the table contains a total width of 300 characters (15 columns with an average width of 15 characters plus some extra for table name, etc.), this would mean it would occupy approximately 1,800,000 bytes (or 1.8 megabytes) of disk storage for that six-month period. Adding the 25% reserve, that gives you a requirement for 2.25 megabytes of storage for that one table. Adding up the other five tables in the database design, the total estimate for this application is about six megabytes of storage required to handle six months of data. This is not an unreasonable guess for a relatively small application, like the one built and used by case study 3.

Relative to the cost of other components, disk storage is usually relatively cheap. The difference between a 40-megabyte and a 60-megabyte drive, for example, is often less than 15% of cost for 50% more storage. Thus, it makes sense to make good guesses about storage required, and then double it, or add at least another 50% (just in case).

Estimating time requirements

Time requirements vary from case to case depending on a number of factors. The most crucial factor, of course, is the expertise of the individuals who are spending the time. The more skilled an individual is, the more likely any design or programming task will be accomplished in an efficient manner, and the more time probably will be conserved.

This time variance is one of the most important reasons to consider utilizing a consultant when developing an application. Even if an in-house person has the skill which would lead you to feel comfortable in supporting an in-house development, the likelihood is that the process will still take longer, in most cases much longer. This is also why consultants tend to charge substantially more than the rate that could be used to bill in-house time: expertise equals time, which equals money. As a rule-of-thumb, system design consultants in today's market will charge a rate that ranges from $75 to $125 per hour depending on the local market, their experience, and the software products they specialize in. You can estimate that the time of an in-house person who is paid $35,000 (plus benefits) will be worth about $25 per hour.

Table 10-1 lists the basic application start-up expense points and presents some rough estimates for those costs, using the requirements developed in case study 2 (EB). The table compares projected start-up hours associated with two different implementation methods. First, the in-house option is explored, in which all development is handled by an expert user or users who are employees of the business. Second, the option to contract out the development process is presented, in which scenario-two time estimates must be considered: in-house time (still a requirement) and consultants' time.

189

Table 10-1 Some start-up expense points and estimated costs. ☞

Assumptions

1. Installation time is ASAP
2. All hardware is installed previously and working.
3. Application development is being managed or performed in-house by a manager with substantial MIS experience.
4. Manager and user time can be charged at $25 per hour.
5. Consultant time is billable at $75 per hour

Expense point	Hours	Cost
Time expenses with in-house development:		
Discover requirements/study feasibility	30	$ 750
Get management on board	20	500
Get users on board	25	625
Evaluate hardware & site requirements	30	750
Develop database design specifications	75	1,875
Build and test application	125	3,125
Install system and train users	30	750
Follow up/review	20	500
Training (10 users @ 5 hrs each)	50	1,250
	405	$10,125
	(Man hours) (10.1 weeks)	(Total $)
Time expenses with consultant development:		
In-house time:		
Discover requirements/study feasibility	20	$ 500
Get management on board	10	250
Get users on board	15	375
Gather input/output documents	15	375
Evaluate consultants	15	375
Manage design and development	10	250
Follow up/review	15	375
Training (10 users @ 5 hrs each)	50	$1,250

Consultant time:

Evaluate hardware & site requirements	10	750
Create database design	30	2,250
Build and test application	50	3,750
Install system and train users	10	750
Follow up/review	15	1,125
	235	$11,625
	(Man hours) (5.8 weeks)	(Total $)

You'll note that the hours involved for a nonprofessional to create a design are substantially more than those for a consultant. In total, the man hours are reduced from 405 to 235, almost in half. You also should take a look at some differences in time that might not be so apparent.

First, the time involved in getting the management and users "on board" can vary substantially; having a professional involved is something like placing a stamp of approval on the process. Suddenly users (and managers) feel more inclined to accept the process rather than pick it apart. Second, note that the consultant time to create the database design depends on in-house time gathering the input and output requirements and the documents to support those requirements. Without that in-house preparation, creating the database design will take at least 50% longer, and the likelihood of redevelopment (changes to the basic requirements) being required is extremely high. Third, make careful note of the assumption that the manager involved has prior experience in MIS (management information systems). Without that experience, it would be difficult to consider an in-house development. Regardless of the developer's expertise, not having a person experienced in managing the process would be like asking for the most unlikely and thorniest problems to emerge.

These are a few of the issues to consider before entering into an agreement with a consultant. In addition, you might keep some other issues in mind. First, your consultant will never know your business as well as you do, and thus a consultant-developed application will never be as reflective of your business as an application developed in-house. Second, an in-house development will likely yield an application that is slower, less flexible, and of lower quality overall; it is unlikely that your in-house expertise will match a consultant's, and the quality, speed, and flexibility of an application are directly related to the developer's expertise. Third, you must consider the effect of this project on in-house resources: an in-house developer will be unavailable to support other projects or requirements (including those already up-and-running) and the stress that probably will result can be quite substantial. And fourth, doing the work in-house doesn't mean just-after-5:00 P.M. The less frequently any developer works on an application, the longer it takes to get anything done.

Hiring a consultant

If you do decide to hire a consultant, at a minimum make sure to cover the following bases.

Be in charge   Take the time to discuss your general business needs first. If the consultant isn't interested in listening, it is a good clue that he won't be receptive to your input throughout the process. Also, be prepared for ongoing interaction. Don't send the consultant off to work and ignore him until the application is complete.

Keep an open mind   You are hiring a consultant for his or her expertise; take advantage of it! Even if you have gone through a design process on your own, listen closely to his/her questions. Questions are often the key to solutions.

Get any agreement in writing   In particular, make sure that you both buy off on the database design, whoever might be responsible for producing it. The biggest threat to a consulting project is a lack of clear specifications. Also, if the agreement includes a range of hours or costs (e.g., 75–100 hours, or $5000–8000 dollars), budget for the upper end of the range. If the project comes in under that, you'll feel good and look good to any manager evaluating what's happening. If not, at least you knew what to expect.

Always check references   No matter what a consultant's PR says, there is no better way to find out if he is legitimate than by asking a prior client. There are many fly-by-night consultants out there, too many of them in the computer consulting business. Make sure that you've got a good chance of getting what you pay for.

Initiating application development

Before spending any money, and certainly prior to entering into any contractual agreement regarding an application, it is crucial that you identify your end result. Having this established will make it possible to discuss your needs with the consultant and should open the needs up for further discussion with other employees in-house. Figure 10-1 describes this as "discovering the requirements," and as outlined in chapter 1 of this book, it is often in the nature of a quest.

It is particularly important to hunt for needs, or at least to touch base, with both the users and the managers who will be involved with the application, particularly if they are two different groups of people. Soliciting agreement on the end result and providing a way to impact the process once the design is underway will go a long way toward making sure that the system is accepted once it is ready to implement. If the goals aren't at least somewhat uniform up-front, you can bet that you won't get uniform usage at the other end.

Don't step off a plank. Conserve your time and money resources until you are thoroughly convinced that the application is worth developing, that it will be cost-effective to bring to implementation, and that you fully understand what will be involved in the process. Once you have arrived at a good understanding of the issues involved, you stand to make a decision that is appropriate to the situation, not a decision driven by anxiety, peer pressure, or "system envy," a dread disease that strikes when you know your competitor has invested in state-of-the-art technology (but you haven't).

Table 10-2 reviews some of these considerations, particularly as they relate to the decision on proceeding with an in-house rather than a contracted application development.

Table 10-2 Comparison of in-house and contracted application development.

Issue	In-House	Contracted
Total out-of-pocket dollars spent	Substantially lower	Substantially higher
Level of business knowledge reflected in system	Excellent	Fair
Quality of result	Fair	Excellent
Flexibility of result	Poor	Excellent
Total time expended	Substantially higher	Substantially lower
RDBMS product knowledge required of manager	High	Low
Knowledge of comparable systems available	Poor	Excellent
Stress level of manager	High	Low

Table 10-2 Continued

Issue	In-House	Contracted
Availability of manager/ developer to other projects	Poor	Excellent
Probability of need to hire temporary support	High	Low

Working through the design process

Once there is agreement as to the end result desired, and you have decided to either forge ahead in-house or contract the job out, the design process commences for real.

Considering off-the-shelf options

Once the design is complete, and you have in your hand a design document that combines the best of theory and practice, it is time to start building a system, right? Wrong. It is only after you have made the investment in the design process that you are in a position to evaluate some of the other application options, particularly those that might be available at substantially lower cost than a custom—just for you—development.

You probably aren't in business alone. In fact, I know of no business that has no competitors, friendly or not. Even the government parallels private industry in many respects. From an application standpoint, this means that there is a good chance that someone else has already gone through the process that you've just emerged from. If your application need is one that spans multiple industries (like the need for an accounting system), it is very likely that you'll be able to locate a previously built system that meets your needs. A previously built application usually is called *off-the-shelf software*, because you might be able to walk into a computer store and buy it right off the shelf. Applications that aren't quite this easy to come by might still be considered off-the-shelf, because you'll still be able to purchase, install, and have the system up-and-running within hours if not days. Compare this to the months it typically takes to get a complete PC-based application up-and-running (years if the project is minicomputer- or mainframe-based) and you can quickly see the cost benefits.

If your application need is specific to your industry, you might find that a generic application probably won't fit it. However, the vertical software market is flourishing; unless you've already done some investigating, you'll probably be surprised to find how many options there are for applications that have been custom designed for someone else in your same business. Obviously, if you can piggy-back on someone else's design headaches, the cost will quickly justify itself. The best place to look for vertical market software is in the trade publications for your industry.

The best part about having completed your design process is that you are truly in a position to assess the off-the-shelf product, not only from a functional standpoint, but from a performance perspective as well. You will be able to look at the application's documentation; better yet, you'll actually be able to talk intelligently with the vendor, carefully assessing whether or not the system will work for you with your specific needs. You won't have to be at the mercy of a software salesman!

You could discover that even if the basic package doesn't work for you, there are some elements of it that will. If the software meets 85% of your requirements, you might be able to live without the missing 15%, at least for some period of time. In fact, many businesses end up regarding software (specifically including applications) as disposable, in the sense that if they can justify the cost in under 24 months, buying a whole new system after 36 months is not unreasonable. You'd probably be surprised to know how many cost justifications arrive at a break-even point less than 24 months out: in the range of 60%, which is substantially more than you might think (MIT 1990).

You also need to investigate whether or not the missing 15% could be made available to you through customization of the software. Many software developers, particularly in the vertical market, are also in the business of customizing their software to individual customer's needs. You'll be surprised to discover how willing most software developers are to help create a custom system. Of course, the moment you move into customization, you begin to run into the same issue that drove you to consider off-the-shelf in the first place: namely, the costs involved. Even so, you might end up with the best of two worlds: customization to support your specific needs, and a price that severely undercuts the potential cost of a completely custom implementation.

Off-the-shelf systems usually range in price from the most simplistic, $99 accounting system, to substantial vertical market applications that run into thousands of dollars. The variance is great because the level of functionality ranges dramatically.

Let's take an example. You have designed a fairly simple application (similar to case study 3: the zoo), and the process took you a total of 50 hours. At an in-house rate of $25/hour, the design cost you $1250. Assuming this is 30% of the overall cost of system development and implementation, this leaves you with a suggested balance of about $4160 that it will cost you to complete the process in-house. You have located a vertical market software that will meet about 80% of your requirements; the cost of this software is $1450. The vendor has estimated that customization to address the "missing" 20% will take 40 hours; at their billable rate of $80 per hour, this adds up to $3200 for a total "off-the-shelf" software cost of $4650. Compared to an in-house cost of $4160, you'll pay almost $500 more for the "off-the-shelf" option, and, of course, that option puts the expense out-of-pocket rather than absorbed by overhead.

Building an application

If you do decide to build your own custom system, you must make sure to provide adequate time for all the steps of the process, particularly on the post-implementation end. In particular, you must not reserve the off-hours to get the development done. Not only will that slow you down dramatically (how coherent are you after a full day's work?), but the decisions you make will not likely be of the quality you should be demanding. Even with substantial on-hours time allocated (and by substantial I mean at least 40% on a weekly basis), you must be prepared for the first round of the life cycle to take months, not weeks. Furthermore, you must be prepared for even your best estimate of the costs involved to be at least 10% low.

On the plus side, however, an application that you have created specifically for your needs normally will be more flexible, more powerful, and better supported by the users than a simple purchase.

Looking at the application environment

Take a close look at the costs that surround the application—the application environment. First, a crucial component is the RDBMS that you select to build your system.

Relational DBMSs range in price depending on the number of users and (to some degree) the differences in the software. A single user version will cost from a low of about $350 to a high of around $800. Multiuser versions usually come in five-user packs and run in the range from $700 to $2000 per pack. Many RDBMSs have optional *run-time* versions which allow an application to be distributed and run on another computer or network without the purchase of another entire RDBMS; this kind of limited functionality is available for $50 to $200 per additional location. Some RDBMSs also support a separate *compiler* product that will allow a user-developed application to be translated into "computer language" and thus perform substantially faster than a nontranslated (compiled) application. Compilers run from $500 to $800 for different RDBMSs.

Evaluating ongoing expenses

Any application will require maintenance. You need to assess the costs and budget for them, or you'll end up playing continuous catch up and being frustrated in the bargain.

Just a brief mention of the costs on the user side of the application: any dollars you devote to enhancing your user skills (e.g., training) will directly affect your other long-term costs.

Maintaining the application environment

The application environment must be maintained in order for you to continue to support the application. Maintenance usually involves both the time and expense of keeping your application environment operational. The maintenance costs that your application depends on may be fairly low, involving simply the vigilance (time) of your system or database administrator, or these costs could be relatively higher and involve an actual change to the fundamental elements of the computer system your application is based on. These kind of changes are addressed briefly below.

There are three major areas that potentially are affected by these changes, which of course parallel those fundamental elements of the application environment:

- Hardware
- Operating systems software
- RDBMS

Upgrading your hardware   Historically, the hardware segment of the computer industry has been the fastest developing. The available hardware tends to be two to three *generations* ahead of the PC on the average user's desk. Each generation represents a dramatic leap forward in the power and speed of the hardware, so two or three generations of difference make for a definite loss of potential for an application.

Even though I have assumed for the purposes of this book that the hardware supporting the application already is up and running, practically speaking it is rarely optimized, and at some point you must consider upgrading. Upgrading usually becomes an issue as a business grows. Even if you have taken into consideration your business plan and any growth you might have projected (see chapter 2), those concerns always are balanced against the cost factor. If building an application to support two years of growth is prohibitively expensive (at least from a hardware point of view), most businesses will opt to build to meet today's requirements, then upgrade as they need to do so.

As the potential of the hardware has increased, its cost has dropped, and so as you consider when to buy you always have to balance not only what you can get in today's market, but what you could get for the same money if you waited until tomorrow's market. In 1991 you can get a 286 machine for under $600, which is remarkable considering that you couldn't buy a PC (the 8086-based original) for less than five or six times that in 1982. So far the industry shows no signs of slowing that type of progress.

Upgrading operating-systems software   One of the biggest questions in the PC industry in 1991 is what *platform* will support PC growth in the next ten years. This term usually refers to the operating system the different software and applications will be supported by. This is of concern in two major areas: the operating system on your PC, and the operating system used to link your PC to others. In 1991 the PC world is still DOS-based, and software and applications are designed to live within the limits of that fairly unsophisticated system. However, other operating systems are making inroads into the PC world, including Unix/Xenix and OS/2. These more advanced systems are designed to take advantage of the capabilities of more advanced hardware. In addition, the release of Microsoft Windows 3.0 has had a dramatic impact on this equation as users choose to remain in the DOS world while upgrading the functionality of their operating system. Windows applications are a different breed from standard DOS applications, because they are designed to utilize Windows' friendlier, more powerful *GUI* (graphical user interface), and also support the use of a mouse.

In 1991 the networked PC world is still substantially based on Novell Netware, although other network operating systems are increasing their market shares. There are a number of issues, many extremely complex, involved in a network operating system, all outside of the scope of this book.

For your purposes, you should just be aware that as improvements to all types of operating systems are made, you will need to evaluate how these improvements might affect your PC, your network, or your application. A shift of operating system is usually quite expensive, because more advanced systems cost exponentially more, where as DOS usually is bundled free with any hardware, Unix or OS/2 must be purchased. In addition, a change to a nonnetwork operating system involves the migration of any currently running applications and retraining of all users. These are often substantial expenses that might run close to 70% of the expenses of the original application development (with the sole exception of the database design process, again usually 30% or so of the overall). However, it might be a justified expense depending on the benefits that might accrue, particularly if those benefits allow a necessary requirement to be fulfilled that previously was not being met.

Changing your RDBMS   As you make different choices regarding your hardware and/or operating-system environments, you might consider re-evaluating your choice of RDBMSs as well. Because, like all software, database management systems are designed to run with specific operating systems, an operating system change might require a change to another DBMS. In addition, RDBMS vendors are progressing at different rates toward the relational model, and as an application grows, those issues could again rear their ugly heads. Migration of an application from one RDBMS to another is also painful to contemplate for reasons similar to those described above: redevelopment costs can be substantial, but again, the benefits could outweigh cost considerations.

Maintaining the application

Even if your application environment is a stable one, you still need to consider the costs associated with ongoing application maintenance. Growth, as always, is a major factor. An implementation of a design that performed suitably when originally installed could become too slow, in which case one of the alternatives is to rework the implemented application, fine-tuning it to meet performance goals.

You also must be aware that once the application has been installed for some period of time and the evaluation phase of the development has occurred, your requirements will be modified. This is a natural process that leads to a better application, one that more closely meets the end result laid out in the beginning of the design process.

This maintenance of the application will cost you. As always, you have the choice of keeping the maintenance tasks in-house, in which case your primary cost will be the time of your in-house developer. You can plan on an average of 10% of your development time being required to support the application on a monthly basis for the first six months, and about 5% thereafter. Major redevelopments are not included in this rough estimate. Taking the example of case study 2 detailed in Table 10-1, you can estimate about 40 hours per month for the first six months at an estimated cost of $1000. You'll see a gradual reduction in support time after that, probably settling to 20 hours per month ($500).

Of course, you also have the choice of contracting out the work. All legitimate consultants provide long-term support to their clients, some at their standard hourly rate, others based on a maintenance schedule drawn up in advance. If you are developing a substantial application (over 100 man-hours) with a consultant, you should consider some kind of maintenance agreement with your consultant that will ensure that support is available when you need it and at a cost you can predict. Again, as a general rule, you might consider a prepaid agreement that provides you with roughly 10% of the initial development time on a monthly basis for the first six months, and another 5% per month thereafter. Taking case study 3's estimate detailed above, 10% of the 115 consultant hours runs 11.5 hours, or about $850 per month for the first six months. Thereafter, you'd probably be safe estimating $400 or so per month for regular ongoing support (see Table 10-3).

Table 10-3 Estimated application maintenance costs. 🐿

Assumptions:
1. Manager and user time can be charged at $25 per hour
2. Consultant time is billable at $75 per hour
3. Time and costs are on a per month basis

Type of maintenance	In-house time	In-house cost	Consultant time	Consultant cost
First six months	40	$1,000	11.5	$850
Post six months	20	$ 500	5	$400

Modifying a design for cost reasons

If these costs seem overwhelming or perhaps out of line with the benefits you anticipate from the development of a new system, it makes sense to take a second look at your end result. Is the application that you propose truly mission-critical? What benefits will accrue if you proceed with the development? Will you be unable to support business growth without it?

Rather than coming up with a yes or a no answer, you'll more likely come up with a maybe, meaning that in some ways the application is critical, but in other ways it will provide nice additions to the way you do business. Many businesses begin to apply priorities to the design elements laid out in the database design, then decide to continue the development with a phased approach, rather than a one-shot deal. This is a very workable way to proceed, because it will allow you to spread the development costs out over a longer period of time, but will provide you the knowledge that each phase, once implemented, will fit neatly into the overall design that was developed right up-front. There won't be a compatibility issue; you'll know where you stand at each step of the way so that you are in a position to reassess continually the cost benefit of continuing to proceed.

In other words, you should never modify a design for cost reasons. The design should reflect the requirements of your business, and a good design should be able to support those requirements for a good long period of time. Even if the continuing development costs prohibit the implementation of the entire design, having the overall document available for phased implementation will always be more beneficial than actually making changes to the fields or tables to reduce the implementation cost. This said, you might in fact consider modifying your design permanently; however, if you do so at this point in the process, at least you're doing so in full knowledge of what you risk: loss of usefulness, compactness, accuracy, or speed.

Is good design worth the cost?

If you've gone through all the details contained within this book and find that you're more overwhelmed than when you started, you're probably in good company. The database design process is not a straightforward one, and a good design does not come cheap. I've always been of the opinion that money paid to a consultant for a database design represents the best value you'll find for those database dollars; at this point you might agree.

However, the costs, although high, should be paid in full knowledge of the benefits that a good relational-database design will bring. This book has focused on the process, but the result is where you'll find your justification. If you design relational tables, you'll get a useful and compact database. If you design detailed integrity constraints, you'll get accurate data. If you consider speed issues where appropriate, you'll get an application that meets your performance requirements. Finally, if you're aware of the costs upfront, you'll be sure to get a cost-effective application.

Appendix

Database Designs for case studies

Case study 1: RTS

Type of business: Financial planning sole proprietorship
Employees: 1 full-time, 1 part-time

Statement of purpose. This financial planner has a need to keep track of what he does and when. He needs to be able to manage his time spent from a historical perspective for billing purposes, and he also needs a way to help him schedule his future time commitments. In addition, he needs to keep better tabs on his client contacts, including who he has talked to, when the contact took place, what recommendations he made, and what follow-up was required.

End result: Manage time
Database design solution: Fig. A-1
Field requirements: Table A-1

Table A-1 Field definitions for case study 1.

Field name	Data type	Domain	Restrictions
Schedule			
Schedule date*	D	No Sundays	
Schedule start date	D		< End date
Schedule end date	D		> Start date
Schedule date printed	D	No Sundays	<= Sched date

Table A-1 Continued.

Field name	Data type	Domain	Restrictions
Appointment			
Appointment number*	N(5,0)		
Appointment date	D	No Mondays	
Appointment start time	T		> 8 AM
Appointment end time	T		< 9 PM
Client ID	N(4,0)	Client table	
Appointment service			
Appointment number*	N(5,0)	Appt. table	
Service code performed*	N(2,0)	Service table	
Hours worked	M(2,1)		
Service			
Service code*	N(2,0)		
Service description	C(25)		
Service rate	M(5)	>$45,<$145	
Client			
Client ID*	N(4,0)		
Client name	C(25)		
Client street address	C(25)		
Client city	C(25)	US only	
Client state	C(2)	US only	
Client zip code	C(10)	City	
Client telephone number	C(12)		
Primary contact name	C(40)		All caps
Secondary contact name	C(40)		All caps
City			
Zip code*	C(10)		
City name	C(25)	US only	
State abbreviation	C(2)	US only	
Invoice			
Invoice number*	N(5,0)		
Invoice date	D		1st or 15th of month
Client ID	N(4,0)	Client	
Total amount due	M(7)		Sum of hrs*rates
Invoice detail			
Invoice number*	N(5,0)	Invoice	
Appointment number*	N(5,0)	Appointment	
Service code performed*	N(2,0)	Service	
Hours worked	N(5,1)		From appt. times

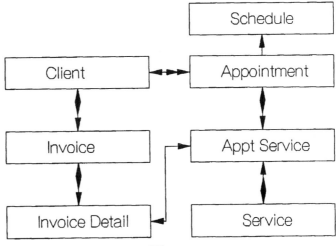

A-1 Database design for case study 1.

Case study 2: EB

Type of business: Purchasing group within a large retail corporation
Employees: 11 full-time (within the group)

Statement of purpose. The purchasing group of a nationwide retail sales company needs to manage the process of buying nonmerchandise supplies for their stores and corporate entities. The group processes requests for supplies that are submitted by various users, forwarding these requests to a vendor or to a corporate warehouse location as indicated.

End result: Manage purchase orders
Database design solution: Fig. A-2
Field requirements: Table A-2

Table A-2 Field definitions for case study 2.

Field name	Data type	Domain	Restrictions
Purchase order			
Purchase order number*	N(4,0)		
Purchase order date	D		
Vendor ID	N(4,0)	Vendor	
Vendor name	C(25)	Vendor	

Table A-2 Continued.

Field name	Data type	Domain	Restrictions
User name	C(40)		All caps
Total purchase order amt.	M(9)		Sum of PO items
PO date closed	D		>PO Date+60
Buyer name	C(40)		All caps
Purchase order item			
Purchase order number*	N(4,0)	Purchase order	
Item number*	N(5,0)	Item	
Quantity	N(5,0)		
Item			
Item number*	N(5,0)		
Quantity ordered	N(9,0)		>=100
Price	M(6)		>1.00,<500
Item description	C(15)		All caps
Vendor item			
Vendor ID*	N(4,0)	Vendor	
Item number*	N(5,0)	Item	
Price	M(9,0)		
Vendor			
Vendor ID*	N(4,0)		
Vendor name	C(25)		Upper & lowercase
Street address	C(25)		
City	C(25)	US city	
State	C(2)	US state	
Zip code	C(10)		Zip plus four
Area code	C(3)	Valid ac	
Phone number	C(8)		Three plus four digits
Purchase request			
Request number*	N(4,0)		
Date requested	D		
Date updated	D		>Date requested
Purchase request item			
Request number*	N(4,0)	Purchase request	
Item number*	N(5,0)	Item	
Quantity	N(5,0)		

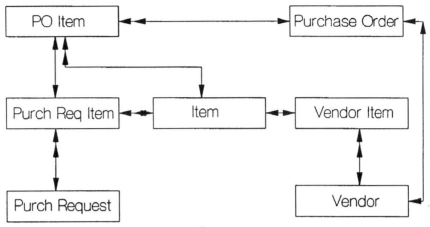

A-2 Database design for case study 2.

Case study 3: MH

Type of Business: Small zoo
Employees: 15 full-time, 9 part-time

Statement of purpose. The owner of this small zoo has a need to keep track of his animals. He needs to know the genealogy for each animal and where it is currently caged in order to plan mating schedules.
End result: Find mates
Database design solution: Fig. A-3
Field requirements: Table A-3

Table A-3 Field definitions for case study 3.

Field name	Date Type	Domain	Restrictions
Animal			
Animal ID*	N(4,0)		Sequential
Animal name	C(20)		
Date of birth	D		
Cage number*	N(4,0)	Cage	
Ancestor			
Animal ID*	N(4,0)	Animal	
Ancestor animal ID*	N(4,0)	Animal	
Type of ancestor*	N(2,0)	Ancestor type	

Table A-3 Continued.

Field name	Date Type	Domain	Restrictions
Ancestor type			
Type of ancestor*	N(2,0)	1,2	
Description of ancestor	C(10)	Mother, father	
Cage			
Cage number*	N(4,0)		
Cage name	C(20)		
Cage building	N(3,0)		<43
Cage row	N(2,0)		<10
Cage level	N(1,0)		<4
Number of spaces total	N(2,0)		
Number of spaces available	N(2,0)		

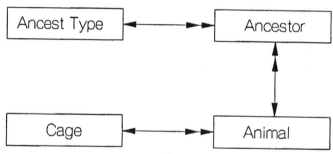

A-3 Database design for case study 3.

🏠 Case study 4: Household

Type of business: N/A
Employees: N/A

Statement of purpose. All you need to do is keep track of the total value for all your depreciable assets so you can give it to your accountant once a year.

End result: Keep list of assets
Database design solution: Fig. A-4
Field requirements: Table A-4

Table A-4 Field definitions for case study 4. 🏠

Field name	Data type	Domain	Restrictions
Asset			
Name of asset	C(30)		Upper & lower
Depreciated value	M(8)		Price–price*DP
Description of asset	C(100)		
Date purchased	D		>1/1/88
Purchase price	M(8)		
Depreciation period	N(4,0)		12-mo. increment
Date sold	D		>date purchased

A-4 Database design for case study 4. 🏠

Asset

Glossary

application   A customized use of database software intended to solve a specific business problem.

application-development software   Database software used to implement or install an application on a PC.

application tasks   Things you need the DBMS to do, usually involving input or output from the database.

atomicity   A quality of a value that indicates it cannot be broken down into components without the loss of its meaning.

autonumbering   A DBMS function that builds a primary key value without the need for user input.

backup   The process of making a copy of the application programs and data (often in some kind of compressed mode).

column   Used interchangeably with field to refer to one descriptive element or attribute of a table (the vertical of the table).

data   Facts (plural), or a fact (singular), meaningless because it lacks context.

database administrator (or **DBA**)   The person who manages the database and applications.

data-based relationships   A quality of a relational database that sets it apart from other types of databases. The data is used to make connections.

data independence   A quality of data that describes the fact that it is accessible through a logical format, and whose users need never know how it is physically stored.

data integrity   The accuracy and validity of data in an application relative to the requirements of the business.

data security   The control the DBMS exerts over who can do what in an application.

data sensitivity   A qualitative assessment of data that describes how secret it is.

data type   A description of a value that the DBMS uses as a way to understand some fundamental qualities of that value.

DBMS (database management system)   Software designed to allow you to manage a wide variety of data types to meet a variety of needs.

disk storage   Magnetic media used to store data permanently.

domain   The pool of values from which actual values in a field might be drawn.

easy-to-use   A DBMS that is intuitive and provide lots of help through detailed menus and well-defined choices, and also screens that look a lot like the physical objects you are already familiar with.

end result   The output of an up-and-running application, and the goal of the application-development process.

entity   Anything that has definite, individual existence in reality or in the mind; anything real in itself.

entity integrity   How accurately a table reflects actual entities in the real world.

export   A translation of data from your DBMS to the format of another software program.

field   Used interchangeably with column to refer to one descriptive element or attribute of a table (the vertical of the table).

field integrity   A measure of the value of a description relative to the actual fact it is describing.

foreign key   A primary key value when used in another table.

form   An image on the computer screen that is used to access data; to input new data, or to look at or modify data that has already been input.

ID (identifier)   The field or fields (or during the design process, the info element) that can be used to identify uniquely each row of a table.

import   A translation of data from another software program into your DBMS.

implementation   The phase of application development during which the design is acted upon (building is begun).

index   A separate and relatively small file used to keep track of values (in the case of a primary index, it tracks primary key values), and that allows a DBMS to access to particular value without searching the table itself.

information   Organized data.

information of value   Information that you are comfortable basing a decision on, or that helps you make a decision.

info element (information element)   An item of information that has not yet been defined or broken down into a specific field or fields.

join   A relational operation that combines tables and brings rows together based on common values.

LAN (local area network)   A group of computers physically linked together with cables, usually utilizing a special operating system to manage the interactions of the multiple users.

life cycle   A development process that spans the life of the system being developed and usually encompasses steps from the identification of the requirements through the installation, training, and evaluation of the system.

link   The potential that exists for a relationship between two tables by virtue of their sharing a common column.

logical table   A table that is conceived by application users to think about and manipulate data.

maintenance   The ongoing work done to an application that is required in order to ensure that it continues to work.

memory (or RAM)   Random access memory, used temporarily to store and process data.

multifield key   A primary key that is applied to multiple fields.

multimedia   Video and audio capabilities.

naming conventions   Rules for naming that you follow as standard practice rather than by necessity.

orphan record   A record once on the "many" side of a one-to-many relationship whose "one" related record has been deleted.

performance   The speed of an application measured against the application's requirements.

primary key   The field or fields used as the identifier for each record in a table.

project   A relational operation by which specified columns are extracted from a table.

program   A set of directions you create and save that tell a DBMS what things to do and in what order.

programming language   Those features of the DBMS that allow you to automate or customize the use of the other features.

query   A technique for asking questions or doing analysis on data managed by a DBMS.

RDBMS (relational DBMS)   DBMS software that (to one degree or another) follows the rules laid out by the relational model.

real-time   A close connection between what is happening in the real world and what is going on in the database.

record   Used interchangeably with row to refer to one occurrence of an object or process within a table (the horizontal of the table).

recovery The process of returning an application to a prefailure state after a problem has occurred.

referential integrity (sometimes **relational integrity**) How accurately the database reflects real-world relationships that exist between different entities.

relational model A set of rules based on relational algebra that describe data structures using mathematical principles. The model describes three aspects of database management: data structures, data integrity, and data manipulation. The data structures are intended to reduce redundancy in data storage, and also to provide efficiency, security, and integrity across databases that are both shared and integrated.

relation A special kind of table that has been modified to follow the rules of the relational model.

repeating group The relational model's term for a feature of an entity that can include more than one value.

restrict A relational operation that extracts specific records from a relational table.

row Used interchangeably with *record* to refer to one occurrence of an object or process within a table (the horizontal of the table).

secondary index An index built on a nonprimary key field.

sophistication The degree of automation of an application that makes use of the system as easy as possible.

sort The arrangement of values into a specified order, usually following the ASCII keycode order.

speed How fast a given task can be accomplished in an application.

system documentation The written-in-English, published version of what the system does, usually including details from the user's perspective as well as from the programmer's perspective.

table A set of columns and rows that describes a single object or process and that is the fundamental data structure of any relational database.

table relationship A path created by data that is used to integrate two tables together.

user A person who works with an application, either to maintain the data or to rely on it, to aid in the decision-making process.

view A combination of fields from tables that acts like a table itself. A view normally is used for a specific input or output process.

Bibliography

Codd, E.F. 1970. A Relational Model for Large Shared Data Banks. *Communications of the Association for Computing Machinery*, 13 (6).

Codd, E.F. 1990. *The Relational Model for Database Management: Version 2.* Reading, MA: Addison-Wesley Publishing Company.

Date, C.J. 1990. *An Introduction to Database Systems: Volume I.* Reading, MA: Addison-Wesley Publishing Company.

Guralnik, David B. ed., 1976. *Webster's New World Dictionary of the American Language.* Cleveland: The World Publishing Company.

Miller, Michael, ed., 1990. *The Info World Test Center Software Buyer's Guide: 1991 Edition.* San Mateo, CA: IDG Books Worldwide.

Mullin, Mark. 1989. *Object-Oriented Program Design with Examples in C++.* Reading, MA: Addison-Wesley Publishing Company.

Parsaye, Kamran, Mark Chignell, Setrag Khoshafian, and Harry Wong. 1989. *Intelligent Databases: Object-Oriented, Deductive Hypermedia Technologies.* New York: John Wiley & Sons, Inc.

Stonebraker, Michael, Jeff Anton, and Eric Hanson. 1987. "Extending a Database System with Procedures." *ACM TODS*, 12 (3).

Tsichritzia, Dionysios and Anthony Klug (eds.). 1987. "The ANSI/X3/SPARC DBMS Framework: Report of the Study Group on Data Base Management Systems." *Information Systems*, 3.

Vang, Soren. 1991. *SQL and Relational Databases.* San Marcos, CA: Microtrend Books.

Ward, M. 1990. *Software That Works.* New York: Academic Press.

Index

Other Bestsellers of Related Interest

BUILDING TURBO PASCAL® LIBRARIES:
Data Entry Tools—*Jeremy G. Soybel*

Create specialized function libraries in the Turbo Pascal environment using this three-in-one guide. Through a series of keystroke-by-keystroke tutorials, you'll develop consistent, easy-to-use interfaces for data management applications. This book presents 60 ready-to-use spreadsheet templates for personal, a basic review of Turbo Pascal and the Environment Menu and specific solutions to everyday data entry and validation problems. 448 pages, 186 illustrations. **Book No. 3734, $24.95 paperback only.**

THE LOTUS® 1-2-3® FINANCIAL
MANAGER: 60 Models—*Elna R. Tymes,*
Charles E. Prael, and Patrick J. Burns

Designed for quick reference, this book presents 60 ready-to-use spreadsheet templates for personal, business, and statistical applications. Each template comes complete with command sequences, cell-by-cell data listings, and screen illustrations. Plus, all model instructions and cell listings are included on a FREE companion disk! This is the largest, most comprehensive collection of spreadsheet templates available today for users of Lotus 1-2-3 Releases 2.01, 2.2, and 3.0. 336 pages, 152 illustrations. **Book No. 3721, $39.95 hardcover only.**

NORTON UTILITIES® 5.0:
An Illustrated Tutorial—*Richard Evans*

Now DOS users and programmers can learn how to take charge of their systems with the new features of release 5.0. Evans covers all the latest utilities and explains the consolidation of older utilities and explains the consolidation of older utilities into compact modules. All illustrations have been changed to reflect the new look of Norton's screens. To ensure technical accuracy, Norton Computing, Inc., has reviewed the book. Each of the utilities is described in detail with its command line switches and parameters. 359 pages, 238 illustrations. **Book No. 3720, $26.95 hardcover only.**

LOTUS® 1-2-3,® RELEASE 2.3:
The Master Reference—*Robin Stark*

Take advantage of the latest features in Release 2.3. Using the unique three-part indexing and cross-referencing system found in her previous encyclopedias, Robin Stark's newest master reference defines and demonstrates all of the commands and functions of Release 2.3. It brings you up-to-date on the new add-ins: Tutorial, Auditor, and Viewer. Also covered are the new graph types and features, including horizontal orientation and 3-D graphs. 496 pages, illustrated. **Book No. 3988, $24.95 paperback only.**

MAC-GRAPHICS® —*Octogram*

This book illustrates clearly the possibilities of producing quality printed matter with the Macintosh. It puts together the key elements in pre-press production, including type, tint, color, grayscale, image, rule, halftone, process color, and graduated color, and shows you how they relate to each other in the process of graphic design. Technical language is kept to a minimum; the visual nature of the book enables even beginners in the field to make fast and accurate graphic decisions. 288 pages, 160 full-color pages plus 128 2-color pages. **Book 3864, $49.95 paperback only.**

MICROSOFT® WORD FOR WINDOWS®
REVEALED—*Herbert L. Tyson*

Tyson concentrates on Word for Windows' more advanced aspects, including the program's WordBASIC macro language, page composition functions, field types and applications, and printer setup procedures. Special sections cover hot-linking to Excel spreadsheets, working around the "Command Not Available" message, and writing single-keystroke macros on the fly. Tyson even includes time-saving macro programs for printing envelopes, turning on "smart quotes," performing multifile search-and-replace, shading graphics on the laser printers, and more. 568 pages, 82 illustrations. **Book No. 3799, $24.95 paperback only.**

LOTUS® 1-2-3® : The Master Reference
—Robin Stark

Now in a new, expanded edition, this book incorporates the same painstaking detail, three-part indexing, and cross-referencing that has characterized all of Robin Stark's work. Stark has updated this bestselling guide to encompass all the new features of Release 3.1, including the new spreadsheet publishing and page layout functions, real-time editing capabilities, mouse support, and scalable fonts. 592 pages, Illustrated. **Book No. 3771, $24.95 paperback only.**

ADVANCED MS-DOS® BATCH FILE PROGRAMMING—2nd Edition—*Dan Gookin*

Here's a thorough introduction to advanced batch file programming that shows you how to customize your system and simplify many of your everyday computing tasks. Featuring more than 50 new batch files and utilities, this book goes beyond the introductory programs offered in other texts and gives you insight into the operation of your computer, including explanations of the newest release of DOS. 528 pages, 107 illustrations. **Book No. 3745, $36.95 hardcover only.**

FROM FORTRAN TO C—*James F. Kerrigan*

James F. Kerrigan shows you how to use your existing knowledge to translate Fortran programming constructs into equivalent C elements. Kerrigan provides an in-depth comparison of Fortran and ANSI C programming concepts, with extensive code examples that illustrate the features of each language. In addition to a parallel analysis of program structures, he examines each Fortran command and defines its counterpart in C . . . describes input, output, and error control mechanisms in both languages . . . and identifies specific C attributes that do not appear in Fortran. 312 pages, 177 illustrations. **Book No. 3661, $34.95 hardcover only.**

WORKING WITH ORACLE® DEVELOPMENT TOOLS—*Graham H. Seibert*

Speed up online inquiries and simplify updates. Make data input and manipulation, menu access, form design, and report formatting and layout easier than ever. Discover new approaches to everything from relational data linking to laser printouts. Do all of this and more with the help of this new desktop reference. It contains detailed instructions for using Oracle's SQL*Forms, SQL*ReportWriter, and SQL*Menu to solve a variety of database management problems. 256 pages, 172 illustrations. **Book No. 3714, $36.95 hardcover only.**

WORDPERFECT POWER: Word Processing Made Easy—2nd Edition—*Jennifer de Lasala*

This guide is the ultimate nontechnical learning tool. Use it to understand 5.1's new features such as optional, mouse-operated pull-down menus and equation-oriented graphics, and to find information on: commands, file management, merging, style sheets, printing, document layout, function key usage, macros, graphics, and much more. 432 pages, Illustrated. **Book No. 3679, $22.95 paperback only.**

WORDPERFECT® 5.1 MACROS
—Donna M. Mosich, Robert Bixby, and Pamela Adams-Regan

Get everything you need to know about macros in any version of WordPerfect through 5.1. Create and use macros to generate form letters, automate mailing list production, index manuscripts, and more! There are more than 300 usable macros covered in this guide (and available on 5.25" disk), with explanations and illustrations on how the macro command language is used. 480 pages, 162 illustrations. **Book No. 3617, $29.95 paperback only.**

LOTUS® 1-2-3® SIMPLIFIED, RELEASE 3.1
—*David Bolocan*

This helpful guide, completely revised to include Lotus® 1-2-3® Release 3.1, has made learning this latest release painless for thousands of users. Bolocan presents over 300 commands, functions, and macros in a logical, step-by-step format—basic commands are explained before more complex ones. You'll explore Release 3.1's built-in publishing functions . . . mouse support . . . scalable fonts . . . real-time editing . . . page layout . . . on-screen formatting . . . and drawing features. Updated illustrations reflect the program's fresh look and improved user interface. 448 pages, 261 illustrations. **Book No. 3772, $19.95 paperback only.**